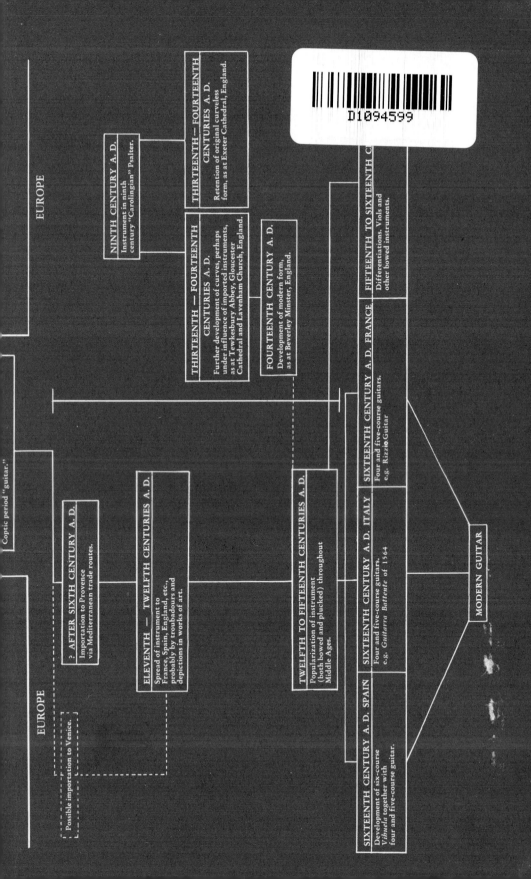

EUROPE

Coptic period "guitar."

EUROPE

Possible importation to Venice.

? AFTER SIXTH CENTURY A. D.
Importation to Provence via Mediterranean trade routes.

NINTH CENTURY A. D.
Instrument in ninth century "Carolingian" Psalter.

ELEVENTH — TWELFTH CENTURIES A. D.
Spread of instrument to France, Spain, England, etc., probably by troubadours and depictions in works of art.

THIRTEENTH — FOURTEENTH CENTURIES A. D.
Further development of curves, perhaps under influence of imported instruments, as at Tewkesbury Abbey, Gloucester Cathedral and Lavenham Church, England.

THIRTEENTH — FOURTEENTH CENTURIES A. D.
Retention of original curveless form, as at Exeter Cathedral, England.

FOURTEENTH CENTURY A. D.
Development of modern form, as at Beverley Minster, England.

TWELFTH TO FIFTEENTH CENTURIES A. D.
Popularization of instrument (both bowed and plucked) throughout Middle Ages.

FIFTEENTH TO SIXTEENTH C[...]
Differentiation. Viols and other bowed instruments.

SIXTEENTH CENTURY A. D. SPAIN
Development of six-course Vihuela together with four and five-course guitar.

SIXTEENTH CENTURY A. D. ITALY
Four and five-course guitars, e.g. Guitarra Battente of 1564

SIXTEENTH CENTURY A. D. FRANCE
Four and five-course guitars, e.g. Rizzio Guitar

MODERN GUITAR

The Illustrated
History of the Guitar

ALEXANDER BELLOW is a Russian born, naturalized United States citizen. A graduate of the Moscow Conservatory, he majored in composition and conducting, and has been awarded the Degree of Doctor of Music with Honors. As a classical guitarist, he has performed here and abroad, both in solo recitals and with chamber groups. Besides being active as a teacher of the guitar, Mr. Bellow's published compositions for the instrument make up an impressive list. He also has transcribed from tablature numerous original compositions for the guitar by early composers, some unknown until now. His *International Anthology* for guitar is published in four languages.

PLATE XXXIII
DETAIL OF WALL PAINTING IN CHURCH OF ST. SEGUNDO AT AVILA, SPAIN
15TH CENTURY

Cf. p. 48

The Illustrated
History of the Guitar

by
Alexander Bellow

FRANCO COLOMBO PUBLICATIONS

A Division of

BELWIN/MILLS PUBLISHING CORP

PRINTED IN U. S. A.

Designed by Robert E. Allen

To My Wife, Mura, and My Daughter, Natasha

Contents

List of Plates

Page

Page

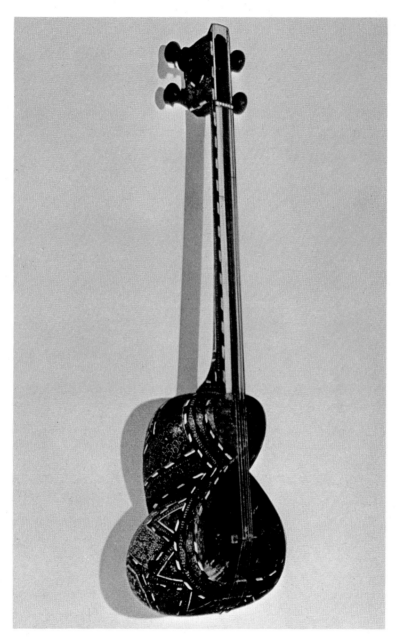

PLATE XXXIV
PERSIAN TAR FROM IRAN
14TH-16TH CENTURY

Cf. p. 55

a FRONT   b BACK

PLATE XXXV
PORTUGUESE VIHUELA SIGNED "ANTONIO DOS SANTOS, VIEN'ZA"
17TH CENTURY

Cf. p. 58

Preface

*F*or me the guitar has always been a beautiful instrument as a medium of expression, and my attachment to it continues to increase with the years. Even as a young conductor in Europe, I was drawn to it; the fascination persisted, and soon the guitar became an indispensable part of my life — a vocation and avocation to which I have devoted a greater part of my energies.

Until I became involved in this history, my primary interest had been with music originally written for guitar. Seeking out manuscripts in dusty vaults, discovering much beautiful guitar music by many wonderful but long-forgotten composers, transcribing their music so that my enjoyment might be better shared, and writing original compositions of my own have all been part of a pleasurable and rewarding preoccupation.

Preparing these compositions for publication meant spending many hours in the office of my friend and publisher, Franco Colombo. With him I spent many pleasant hours discussing the guitar, its lore, its history, its future.

This book is a product of those conversations. The day I was commissioned to write it was the beginning of years of research prompted both by curiosity and love for the instrument.

The more I delved into the history of the guitar, the more convinced I was in my contention that the guitar is not just an appendage to the family of string instruments. Its musical role is more than that of an instrument to be plucked and strummed as an accompaniment to songs and ballads. I hold to this argument despite the belief of many people who (until recently) have insisted on relegating the guitar to a subservient status. But the amount of serious music written for the instrument indicates that the guitar is capable of far greater musical expression, on par with the violin or the piano.

Berlioz taught the guitar and composed with its help. Paganini was as much a master of the guitar as he was of the violin and composed much music for the instrument. Schubert, Rossini and Saint-Saëns are but a few of the many distinguished composers who played the guitar and used it as they composed. Louis XIV, Benjamin Franklin, Mary Queen of Scots, and Catherine of Aragon are some of the historical figures who played the instrument; Henry VIII had twenty-one guitars in his private collection.

The instrument's popularity, which has increased tremendously in recent times, has led to an ever increasing number of guitar recitals and recordings every year. More and more musicians are choosing the guitar as their medium of expression. Unfortunately, however, these developments have not resulted in the publication of a comprehensive history of the guitar. It is with the aim of taking the first tentative step in this direction that this book was written.

I would be neglecting a very pleasant duty if I failed to mention the many friends throughout the world who have given me invaluable assistance from the beginning of my venture. I am especially indebted to the many private collectors, archaeologists, curators, librarians and archivists of various museums too numerous to mention individually, and without whom the preparation of this book would have been an extremely arduous undertaking. I wish to acknowledge my gratitude to them, as well as the following:

The staff of the Ashmolean Museum in Oxford, the Louvre Museum in Paris, and the Museo Municipal de Instrumentos de Barcelona.

Mr. Desmond Hill, Esq. of William E. Hill & Sons, Bond Street, London.

Mr. Henry G. Fisher, Curator of the Egyptian Department, and the entire staff of the Near Eastern Department of the Metropolitan Museum of Art in New York.

Mr. Burhan Tezçan of the Archaeological Museum in Ankara, Turkey.

Sr. Giulio Ascarelli, Mr. George H. Orenstein and Mr. Joseph Pole, who have been instrumental in securing photographic material.

Sr. Juan Riera of Lérida for his help in doing research on the guitar in Spain.

To Jonathan Chaves for his valuable assistance in preparing the manuscript; to Roger H. Lewis, who made it possible for me to obtain much indispensable photographic material.

Last, but not least, I wish to thank my wonderful wife, Mura, for her interest, encouragement and help.

A. B.

Prologue

*T*he historian who chooses the guitar for his subject must contend with a seemingly insurmountable problem since source materials, particularly those prior to the sixteenth century, are extremely scant; evidence to support the theories he must formulate are difficult if not impossible to obtain. This lack of information constitutes one of the main reasons for writing this book. For gaps in knowledge move the mind to action, and the little known gives impetus to exploration.

In any study of culture and the arts, the work of archaeologists and scholars of ancient civilizations is of great value. Trustees, curators and personnel of many museums and institutes throughout the world have made available to me precious and rare photographs of original carvings, plaques and art objects pertinent to the history of the guitar.

After considerable study, and after a process of careful elimination, it appeared that the earliest instrument related to the guitar was one represented in several Babylonian relief-sculptures of the second millenium B. C. (*Plates III and IV*) It was, however, quite obvious that this was an already highly developed instrument, that it had been the product of many years of growth and change. A fresh challenge, therefore, presented itself: that of tracing this instrument's ancestry.

Since the Babylonians derived much of their culture from the Sumerians, Sir Leonard Woolley's famous excavations of the Royal Cemetery in the ancient Sumerian city of Ur offered a number of important clues. Here, in ruins that date back to c. 2500 B. C., was abundant evidence of a rich and brilliant culture at its peak: remarkably constructed temples which showed the Sumerians' familiarity with architectural principles that modern man still finds useful; furniture, chariots, boat models, beads and jewelry in silver, lapis lazuli, marble, crystal and agates of exquisite colors and high polish; copper mirrors, golden toilet sets, tweezers, pottery and metal objects of all kinds. Among these were articles especially significant to my search — the ancestors of the Babylonian guitar, the first string instruments found anywhere in the world.

These can be divided into two general types: those which Sir Woolley calls "harps" and those which he calls "lyres."

The most outstanding example of the first type has become known as "Queen Shub-Ad's* Harp". *(Plate I.)*

PLATE I
"QUEEN SHUB-AD'S HARP"
C. 2500 B.C.

*also known as Pu'abi

This beautiful instrument had a rectangular wooden soundbox decorated with gold and inlaid with mosaic of red stone, white shell and lapis lazuli. At the time of the excavation the wooden portions had decayed. The soundbox was so perfectly impressed in the surrounding earth (the surviving parts, the gold decorations and inlays imbedded in what probably were their original positions) that a restoration of the instrument was eventually completed.

The most exquisite ornament on this "harp" was the golden head of a bull, attached to the front of the soundbox. *(Plate II)* For us, the most pertinent factor to note is the definite articulation of soundbox and neck, as opposed to the continuous curve of the ancient bow-shaped harps.

The lyres also had a soundbox almost invariably decorated with an animal's head, but they had two uprights which supported a crossbar at the top, to which the strings were attached. These instruments varied in size; one of the graves, for example, yielded four lyres of different dimensions, each decorated with an animal head. One had a golden bull's head; another, a silver cow's head, and one, which was boat-shaped, had the complete figure of a stag. Except for this last instance, the rectangular soundbox seemed to be a highly abstract representation of the animal's body.

It seems that the choice of a particular animal's head corresponded to the size of the instrument and the sound quality expected of it. Inscriptions by the famous governor Gudea of Lagash describe a harp which he had presented to a temple. When played, the instrument, which was decorated with a bull's head, bellowed like a bull.

PLATE II
"QUEEN SHUB-AD'S HARP"
Detail of soundbox

The varying sizes and sounds of the lyres could indicate ensemble playing or ancient chamber music of some kind. This in turn would suggest some form of polyphony in the Sumerians' music. It is unfortunate that, to our knowledge, examples of their musical notation (if it existed at all) have not been found.

A number of animal heads, unattached to anything, were also found in these excavations. Among these was a human head with horns protruding from it. This was, perhaps, the most interesting and important in the group. Measuring about four and a half inches high, horns included, it was the smallest of the lot and the only one of its kind discovered. There is evidence to support the belief that this represented a deity, and that at one time it adorned a musical instrument. (The suggestion that the head decorated furniture and not a musical instrument is refuted by the almost exclusive use of the lion's head — a royal insignia — for this purpose.) But its uniqueness raised a question: what instrument? A lyre? A harp? Its size excluded it from strict and categorical classification.

If we consider the proportion of head-to-lyre as being relatively consistent (and this conclusion is supported by observation of other lyres), then the lyre to which the deity's head was once attached would have to be only about seventeen or eighteen inches tall. But the smallest lyre found (really the imprint of a decayed lyre in the ground from which a plaster cast was made) is approximately thirty-six inches in height, or twice as high as the hypothetical instrument with the deity's head; its bull's head, which has survived, is nine and a half inches tall, horns included. It is, therefore, extremely doubtful that the instrument which the deity's head once adorned was a lyre.

It is unfortunate that this instrument could not have been located. Perhaps it was made entirely of perishable wood, and its smallness and lightness did not allow for incrustation; however, certain assumptions may be made based on what is actually known: priests in Babylonia played on a guitar-like instrument as they sang and danced during religious ceremonies. Since the deity's head could very well have fitted onto the end of the neck of one such instrument, it is conceivable that that was where it in fact belonged, and that this instrument had a sacred or liturgical function. Since the Babylonians after conquering Sumer absorbed much of its culture, it is probable that this guitar-like instrument existed in Sumer prior to its adoption by the Babylonians.

When all this evidence is considered as a whole, a certain trend of development, albeit sketchy, may be proposed.

The most ancient of string instruments was probably the bow-shaped harp, which may have been inspired by the twang of the hunting bow, a sound familiar to all who have observed or participated in archery. A cylinder seal found in Ur shows such an instrument with four strings, high enough to be played by a standing figure.

After this, large lyre-like instruments came into being. As can be seen from more cylinder seals also found in Ur, these had five strings.

Since a parallel evolution in Egypt bears out the theory that such instruments gradually became smaller in the course of their evolution, it would be reasonable to conclude that the instruments found in the Royal Cemetery — smaller and with strings numbering from eleven to seventeen — represented a later stage of development. These instruments did not necessarily replace one another, but rather, increased the variety of musical instruments at the time.

"Queen Shub-Ad's Harp" in particular, representing the general type of neck harps, bears certain similarities to the guitar-like instruments of the future. It had a soundbox of wood and a definitely separate neck. The essential difference is that this neck was vertical, whereas that of the guitar is horizontal. However, if we assume for the sake of argument a gradual lowering of the neck to the horizontal position, this harp may be seen as the earliest known direct ancestor of the guitar.

The increasing complexity of the music played probably accounted for the change in the position of the neck. As the musicians of the ancient world plucked the open strings of their instruments, they probably became aware of the phenomenon which we now know as harmonics or overtones. As these became more and more popular, a desire for wider tonal variety and for greater facility in performance may have encouraged the musicians to experiment by stopping the strings against the neck. Naturally, the lower the neck the easier it would be to stop the strings. As stopping became a practice, the number of playable notes increased. Lowering the neck was certainly an alternative more practical than multiplying the number of strings, a process which would eventually have required an instrument of prohibitive proportions — or the modern day harp's skillful engineering which, we know, was non existent at that time.

Thus we see that our small deity's head, if we accept its position as being at the end of a horizontally placed neck, was an important link in a chain of developing instruments.

These changes must have begun as early as the third millenium B. C. The highly developed Babylonian instruments of 1900-1800 B. C. represented an evolution spanning several hundred years.

The highly theoretical nature of all this must be re-emphasized. Its justification lies in the need to supplement our present limited knowledge by drawing a recognizable picture. Meanwhile, we wait for archaeologists to supply us with the missing pieces in our puzzle. With this as starting point, we can then proceed to our discussion of the Babylonian "guitars".

The Illustrated
History of the Guitar

CHAPTER *1*

The Ancient Near East

*I*t may be said that the history of the guitar began to unfold in the ancient Near East. There, the archaeologists found instruments and representations of them that served as landmarks or guideposts in the relatively uncharted territory of the guitar's beginnings.

From Queen Shub-Ad's era (2500 B. C.), to the time of the first evidence of musical instruments in Babylonia (1900 B. C.), stretched a period of some six-hundred years, centuries of obscurity unrelieved by any discoveries of musical significance. But historical events within this span of time, and artifacts from subsequent Babylonian excavations, support the inference that the musical instruments of Queen Shub-Ad's era continued to exist and to develop.

History informs us that the Akkadians from the northern part of Mesopotamia conquered the Sumerians, whose culture they then adopted and modified. Sumer thus became part of the Akkadian Empire, established and ruled by King Sargon I. Despite the conquest, however, Sumer regained a measure of autonomy which allowed its culture to flourish once again, principally in the city of Ur. The Third Dynasty of this great city lasted for over a hundred years, until Babylonian power absorbed Mesopotamia (1900 B. C.) and unified the entire region into what eventually became known as the Great Babylonian Empire (1800 B. C.). Its founder and ruler was the famed King Hammurabi.

Excavations at Ur have yielded clay plaques and documents which bear witness to the importance of music in the religious and social life of ancient Babylonia. Religious ritual, particularly, almost always required chants, musical instruments and dances. These varied according to the occasion and the ceremony attached to it. Some called for accompaniment by large drums, others for flutes, and still others for string instruments. Less frequently, mixed ensemble was required. A list of chants has survived which shows specific instrumental requirements for each chant. Obviously, therefore, a variety of instruments were in use at the time.

The training of musicians and chanters was long and rigorous, and special "colleges" attached to temples existed to serve this purpose. In addition, intensive rehearsals preceded every performance at ceremonial functions.

Evidently musical instruments played an important and essential role in religious ritual. A description of one rite might serve as illustration.

Babylonian religion required that the statues of gods and objects associated with the cult be consecrated and blessed. Among these objects were musical instruments used for worship. The *âshipu,* priest-representative of the gods of magic, officiated. He recited the prescribed formulae while touching statues and objects with some appropriate implement. It was the belief that this ceremony would eventually bring to life the statues and musical instruments that the *âshipu* had touched.

Among the artifacts excavated from Babylonia, the most relevant to our subject were the clay plaques dated 1900-1800 B. C. These showed nude figures playing musical instruments, some of which bear a general resemblance to the guitar. *(Plate III)* Archaeologists have advanced the opinion that the figures represented priests and certain facts do bear out this assumption.

Sumerian mythology, absorbed by Babylonian culture, formed the basis of many requirements for the Babylonian priesthood. According to these requirements, the successors of Enmenduraki (who originated the practice of these rites) had to be outstanding specimens of manhood, in perfect physical condition and without so much as a blemish on the skin. They were to complete years of study and training before undergoing special initiation rites. For these, the head and entire body of each *bârû* or high priest

2

must be thoroughly shaven in accordance with ceremonial directive: "The barber hath done his handiwork upon him." They would thereafter enjoy the special protection of the gods, and their task would be to worship all the deities in the temples. They were also to be interpreters of letters and laws, and, as such, were to take an oath of loyalty to the king.

PLATE III
BABYLONIAN CLAY RELIEF FROM ESHNUNNA
Representing a high priest (bârû) playing guitar-like instrument
C. 1900 B.C.

If we can, therefore, assume that the bald, nude figures were in fact priests, and that their activities were exclusively of a religious and solemn nature (church and state in ancient Babylonia being a unity), then the guitar-like instruments which they are portrayed as playing could very well be sacred, or would at least have performed a sacred function.

The adoption of Sumerian culture by the Babylonians, the previously mentioned possibility of similar guitar-like instruments in Sumer, and the presence of such highly developed instruments in Babylonia so shortly after its rise to power corroborate our theory: that the instruments from Queen Shub-Ad's time survived and were generically the same (though perhaps minimally changed) as those eventually found in the hands of Babylonian priests.

Close examination of the instrument *(Plate III)* shows it to have a distinctly differentiated body and neck. Its back is undoubtedly flat; the manner in which it rests against the priest's chest precludes the possibility of its being bowl-shaped. Although it is not possible to determine whether the strings are plucked with fingers or a plectrum, it is clear that the right hand does the plucking. The proportion of neck to body is remarkably similar to that found on the modern guitar. This similarity is made more striking by the fact that other ancient string instruments have much smaller soundboxes in relation to their necks.

Evidently this instrument was highly developed, but from the standpoint of guitar-like instruments in general its primitive state is apparent from its straight sides. This feature and the flat back seem to have persisted for about three thousand years. Sculptures of similar instruments on the "Gate of Glory" at the Santiago de Compostela Cathedral in Spain *(Plates XXVIII and XXIX)* tend to support this point.

The number of strings on this instrument would, of course, be of great interest to us. But it is not quite clear whether the sculptor who executed the plaque meant to represent the strings by the grooves, or by the raised portions.

Another plaque, a better preserved one, found on the site of the old Babylonian city of Ishali *(Plate IV)* provides more conclusive information. A priestess is shown playing the same type of instrument, and this allows us to date this find to the time of King Hammurabi, (c. 1800 B.C.) who, in his famous code, defined the position of women as co-equal to that of men.

PLATE IV
BABYLONIAN TERRA COTTA RELIEF FROM ISHALI
Representing a high priestess playing guitar-like instrument
C. 1800 B.C.

Almost the entire neck of the instrument is visible. Two tassels and knots which hold the strings at the upper end of the neck strongly suggest that there were at least two strings on this instrument. A slight bulge hints at a third tassel and knot; therefore, at the possibility of a third string. The clarity with which all five fingers of the priestess's left hand are shown leads to another interesting observation: the thumb, protruding from behind the neck of the instrument, was probably used to press the strings, a practice common up to the 19th century on our modern guitar.

As has been noted, these instruments used by the high priests and priestesses closely resemble the modern guitar and may be considered direct predecessors of it.

5

It would also be safe to assume that these instruments were widely used. The relief featuring the *bârû* was found in Eshnunna (modern Tell-Asmar), a former Sumerian city which was at the height of its power in c. 1830 B. C., the plaque with the priestess figure was found in Ishali, an ancient city where quantities of fine art work were discovered. The fact that these two cities were thirty-five miles apart indicates these instruments were in use in most temples of Babylonia.

Two other plaques in the Louvre Museum in Paris *(Plates V & VI)* show naked, bearded minor priests playing instruments similar to those discussed above but with soundboxes that were considerably smaller. The grooves along the neck obviously represent strings. There are two of these, as well as two knots and two tassels. By moving the knots up or down the neck while pulling on the tassels, the strings were tuned and held secure in the desired position.

A number of variants on these instruments have been seen on reliefs, most notably in the shape of the sound-boxes. Some were oval, others were trapezoidal with rounded corners. The necks were generally long. Apparently, aesthetic as well as functional considerations influenced these variations. Such differences in size and shape produced differences in tone quality; specific functions required specific instruments. Thus, to the minor priests, whose religious duties involved more active participation not only in playing but also in dancing, the smaller instrument was the more appropriate and convenient.

These necked instruments were not the only ones used by the Babylonians. A relief excavated at Eshnunna and dating from about 1800 B. C. *(Plate VII)* shows a harp similar in basic structure to "Queen Shub-Ad's Harp" from Ur. The essential difference is that the neck has been shortened so that the harp could then be played with the soundbox in a vertical position. Evidently the evolution from harp to necked instruments of the guitar type did not follow one single line. There was, more likely, a branching off in a number of directions, so that while variants came to being along the way, the harp, as such, continued to survive with only minor variations.

Running parallel to Babylonian culture of this period was that of the Hittites, the "sons of Heth". These people lived in Anatolia (modern Turkey), north of Babylonia.

PLATE V
BABYLONIAN CLAY RELIEF
Representing a minor priest playing a string instrument of small size
C. 1900 B.C.

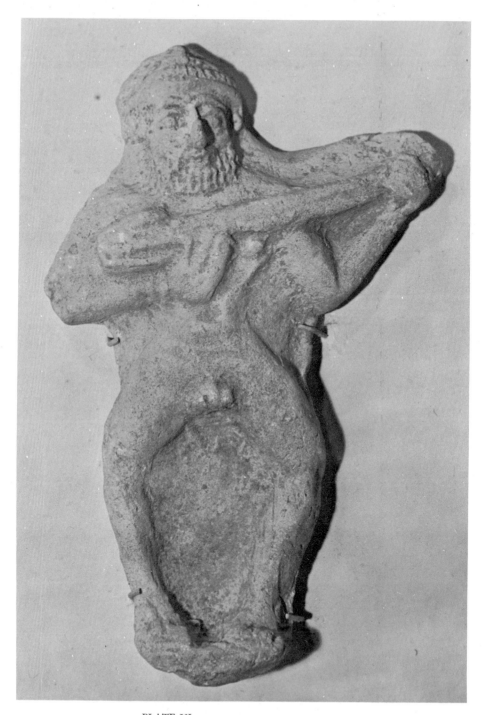

PLATE VI
BABYLONIAN CLAY RELIEF
Representing a minor priest playing a string instrument of small size
C. 1900 B.C.

They were first unified under King Labarnas, who rose to power in 1680 B. C., and whose name became the title for subsequent rulers. Under his reign the social and political structure of the Hittite Empire was established. Expansion, both eastward and westward, followed until finally, in the reign of King Murshilish I (1620-1590 B. C.), the Hittites rose to prominence and consolidated their position as a leading power in the Near Eastern world.

Relatively little is known of these people, but what is

PLATE VII
BABYLONIAN TERRA COTTA RELIEF FROM ESHNUNNA
Representing a musician playing a vertical harp
C. 1800 B.C.

9

known points to their being artistic craftsmen and pro-
ficient in the use of metal.

Hittite artists left many monuments, gates, palaces,
walls and columns decorated with stone carvings and
reliefs. One of these, dating from c. 1300 B. C. and found
on the Sphinx Gate of Alacahüyük, represents two musicians, one of them playing a truly remarkable guitar-
like instrument. *(Plate VIII)*

Two tassels hang from the upper part of the neck,
indicating that the instrument had two strings. These
the musician plucks with a plectrum attached by a cord
to the soundbox. On the soundboard are punctures undoubtedly meant to function as sound holes — five by
each side of the neck, which extends along the length of
the soundbox.

The most fascinating feature of the instrument is the
cross hatchings, clearly visible along the neck. Remember-
ing the Hittites' expertise as metal workers, perhaps it
would not be presumptuous to suppose that these were,
if not actually metal frets, their prototypes. If so, we have
in this relief the first representation of a fretted instrument.

This "guitar" seems to have played an important and
popular role in Hittite social and religious life. The instrument is prominently displayed in Hittite reliefs depicting religious and royal occasions: portraying gods, god-
desses, kings, horseback riders and banquet scenes.

The proportion of the instrument to the Hittite musician's body closely approximates the proportion of the
modern guitar to the size of the average contemporary
man. In this respect the similarity of the two instruments
to each other is truly striking.

This Hittite instrument could only have been the result
of many centuries of development. Whether this instrument originated and developed exclusively within the
confines of Hittite culture, or whether it was transplanted
to this region from elsewhere, can only be a subject for
conjecture. Even though there were occasional Babylonian
influences on Hittite art, these influences were slight. A
clear and definitive pattern of evolution is extremely difficult, if not impossible, to establish because climatic conditions and geographic circumstances conspire against the
survival of wooden instruments. The bulk of evidence
must, therefore, be drawn from stone carvings, clay

plaques, metal works and reliefs. In the task of locating these, archaeologists are constantly frustrated, their labors made more time consuming, for the valley between the Tigris and Euphrates was frequently flooded by these great rivers. When these overflowed their banks in 1831, seven thousand Baghdad homes perished in a single night. In May, 1967, thirty-two villages were severely damaged.

PLATE VIII
HITTITE STONE RELIEF FROM ALACAHÜYÜK
*Representing a musician playing a guitar-shaped
instrument*
·C. 1300 B.C.

Besides Babylonian and Hittite cultures, there were others spread throughout Asia Minor which showed evidence of guitar-like instruments similar to those played by the minor Babylonian priests. These have been noted in Assyria, Susa, and Luristan.

An interesting relic from this last site, situated on the Persian plateau, is a *situla* in repoussé metal work. *(Plate IX)* This cup, dated 700 B. C., shows a banquet scene with three participants. One of them plays a string instrument with a long neck, apparently entertaining a royal personage who is in the act of taking a drink. Since the hammering of the cup is not particularly detailed, only

11

PLATE IX
REPOUSSÉ METAL SITULA FROM LURISTAN (IRAN)
Representing a musician playing a string instrument with neck
C. 700 B.C.

the general features of the instrument are recognizable, but these suffice for identification.

From Susa, we have a yellow stone relief (c. 1100 B. C.) depicting a procession. The figures carry animals, plants, and musical instruments of guitar-like appearance.

History recounts constant invasions and counter-invasions among the nations of the Near East. The geographical proximity of the Babylonians, Sumerians, Akkadians, Hittites, and Assyrians made it almost inevitable that these warlike peoples should often be engaged in battle. In the interim periods they traded with each other, interchanged court musicians, exchanged gifts, and occasionally inter married. This led to some absorption of each other's culture. Conquerors influenced the conquered and vice-versa. The components of culture — ideas, modes of life, artifacts — crossed and re-crossed regional boundaries. Through such means the various necked instruments were disseminated all over the Near East. Eventually they found their way to Egypt where they combined with that country's native instruments and continued to evolve into the more immediate ancestors of the guitar.

CHAPTER *2*

Egypt

*E*gypt, seat of one of the world's oldest and greatest civilizations, has given us a rich legacy of monuments, artifacts and relics by which we may gain an insight not only into its own and neighboring cultures but into parts of ours as well.

Since time immemorial the Egyptians have believed in life-after-death, in the ability of the spirit to enjoy in eternity such worldly goods as can be buried with the departed. Hence, they mummified their dead and interred them in mighty tombs calculated to defy erosion and time. Until c. 1600 B. C., these were constructed in the form of pyramids. After this time, they took the form of tunnels or "syringes" dug into the sides of mountains. The durability of these structures helped preserve everything that was sealed within them. Thus, when archaeologists gained access to the tombs many centuries later, they found in a remarkably preserved state not only mummies, but also a quantity of worldly goods and decorations: musical instruments, relief sculptures, wall paintings, toilet articles, jewelry and the like. The first three items are the principal sources of information concerning Egyptian musical life.

In the earliest days, the only plucked string instrument in Egypt was the bow-shaped harp. It had an oval soundbox which also served as the base of the instrument. Judging from the great number of reliefs and wall paintings in which it was represented, it was highly popular both as a solo and ensemble instrument.

PLATE X
EGYPTIAN RELIEF
C. 2500 B.C.

A particular relief from the Fifth Dynasty (c. 2500 B. C. *Plate X)*, found in Sakkareh, shows a musician playing a bow-shaped harp with six tuning pegs. Another relief from the Fourth Dynasty, discovered in the tomb of Idou, shows a group of five musicians, each playing a harp. If the different positions of the musicians' hands on the strings indicate that they were playing different notes, some kind of true ensemble music must have existed in Egypt then. Great numbers of reliefs show performers on bow-shaped harps in consort with flutists and vocalists.

Apart from the depiction of the bow-shaped harps on reliefs, there was actually one such instrument found at El Assiri Cemetery in Thebes. *(Plate XIa)* A comparison of its date (1900 B. C.) with that of the Fifth Dynasty relief mentioned previously leads to the conclusion that bow-shaped harps of the same type had been in use at least seven-hundred years before.

The "El Assiri harp", which is now in the Metropolitan Museum of Art in New York, was similar in shape to those shown in the above reliefs, although of a lesser height. Originally it also had six strings. According to archaeologists, however, modifications had been made in ancient times to allow the use of only five strings: three single and two double. This was the first evidence of double strings. The bridge, across the soundbox, was notched to anchor the strings, and the soundbox itself was covered with a drumhead of rawhide. Both this and the neck were once colored red; the bridge was black.[*]

[*]This instrument was carefully examined by the author.

16

The description of these instruments reveals two essential changes: one, the decrease in size; the other, the reduction in the number of strings. These constitute the evolutionary trend that will be followed by subsequent instruments.

An instrument dated three-hundred years later (c. 1600 B.C.), and now owned by the Oriental Institute of Chicago, has a neck that has been lowered considerably. *(Plate XIb)* It rises at an angle only fifteen degrees removed from a perfectly horizontal alignment with its soundbox. This made it easier to press the strings against the neck at the upper end. A greater

PLATE XIa
EGYPTIAN BOW-SHAPED HARP
C. 1900 B.C.

variety of pitches, therefore, became possible. Thus, the number of strings was reduced to four. The length of this instrument was less than the height of the "El Assiri harp". Its soundbox was also covered with a membrane. Traces of the pressure exerted on it by the fastening cords are still visible. Neck and soundbox (at the top of which is attached a bridge to which the strings were fastened) were still carved from a single piece of wood and were differentiated only by the angular rise of the neck.

The general construction of this "harp" is similar enough to that of the previous instruments to allow its classification under the same species, but this instrument was evidently in a later stage of development. At the same time it differed markedly enough from its predecessors so that it can no longer be considered a true bow-shaped harp. Its proper position is therefore in the transitional stage between the bow-shaped instruments and those with slightly curved but separately articulated necks. That part of the evolutionary trend involving a decrease in size was in fact largely due to the gradual lowering of the neck. This originally was a continuation

17

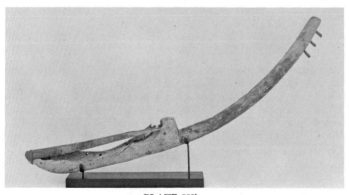

PLATE XIb
EGYPTIAN NECKED INSTRUMENT
C. 1600 B.C.

of the bow and only later became a separate piece attached horizontally to the soundbox.

Another instrument *(Plate XII),* with general characteristics similar to the one described above, is now in the Hamburg Museum. Its neck had been broken and the exact angle at which it was attached to the body cannot be accurately determined. However, it was probably less bent than it now appears to be. The soundbox is covered with a piece of plastered linen which is decorated with reddish-brown stripes. Around the rim are several small sound holes. The strings were fastened to a cylindrical protrusion at the end of the soundbox. The precise date and origin of this instrument are unknown, but it is quite clear that it belongs to one of the branches developed from bow-shaped harps.

The evolutionary trend under discussion finally culminates in a crucially important instrument that, for the first time, has a perfectly straight and horizontal neck. *(Plate XIIIa)* It dates from c. 1500 B.C. and is named after Har-Mosĕ, the Egyptian singer and musician in whose grave it was found.

Har-Mosĕ was the favorite musician of Sen-Mūt, architect to the great Queen Hat-Shepsut (crowned 1503 B.C.). Sen-Mūt was one of the most famous men of his time. In accordance with Egyptian custom, he was buried with those objects that he wished to have with him in the afterlife. In addition to his monkey and horse, he had arranged to have Har-Mosĕ mummified for burial in the vicinity of his own tomb. This was still being carved out of rock when Har-Mosĕ died. He was therefore buried beneath the pile of limestone that was gradually filling

PLATE XII
EGYPTIAN NECKED INSTRUMENT. DATE UNKNOWN

up the nearby gully. His coffin, though that of a poor man, bore a sign of his master's esteem. Instead of the complete anonymity fit for one of a low social class, it was inscribed with name and title, "Singer, Har-Mosĕ".

For Sen-Mūt, the realization of his plans meant that he was at last fully equipped to enjoy the after life, his favorite musician and his pets by his side. For later generations, his arrangements afforded a glimpse into matters of considerable significance. The monkey served as a reminder of the Egyptian belief in the ape as sacred to the ibis-headed Thoth, scribe of the gods. The horse, at the time a recent arrival from Asia Minor, was the first mummified horse discovered in Egypt. And Har-Mosĕ, having brought his musical instrument with him to the grave, provides us with an important link in the evolutionary chain which now concerns us.

19

It is remarkable that this delicate instrument should have withstood the weight of the stones under which it had remained buried for more than three-thousand years. Despite some damage — the sound-board had split at two points owing to shrinkage, and the three gut strings had almost disintegrated — the instrument was fairly well-preserved. The beautifully polished soundbox, probably of cedar wood, was intact, as also was the plectrum attached to it by a long cord.

The soundbox is elongated-oval in shape. The cylindrical neck passes through a series of slits in the rawhide, which had been punctured to create six small sound holes. The rawhide, covering the soundbox, had been stretched over this while still wet so that, upon drying, it would exert enough pressure to hold the neck firmly in position. At the tip of the soundbox are three more slits to receive the gut strings and a pocket to fasten the neck. Tension on the strings was regulated by a rope which had been tightly wound around knots of linen. The linen in turn was attached to the strings. The rope then was moved up and down the neck of the instrument in order to change the pitch. *(Plate XIIIb)* The total length of the instrument is forty-seven inches. Judging from paintings and reliefs (all of which, incidentally, postdate the actual Har-Moše instrument), there were at one time two bridges on the rawhide.

Looking back through the line of evolution from the Har-Moše instrument to the bow-shaped harps, we see a development that is continuous and independent of similar developments in Sumer and Babylonia. It is therefore clear that while influences from the Near East may have played their part, the straight-necked instruments in Egypt were the result not of importation but of changes that took place within the country itself.

After the reign of Queen Hat-Shepsut, King Tuthmosis III (1504-1450 B. C.) led several campaigns in the Near East, capturing Megiddo in 1481 B. C. and raiding such important centers as Subaro, Ketna, and Niy. Eventually the Egyptians came to dominate practically the entire Near East. Delegations from Babylon, Assyria, Mitanni, the Hittites, Cyprus and Crete were received in Egypt. As a result, an instrument similar in general construction to that of Har-Moše's found its way into the country.

Reliefs and paintings show this to have had an oval soundbox smaller than that of the Har-Moše instrument.

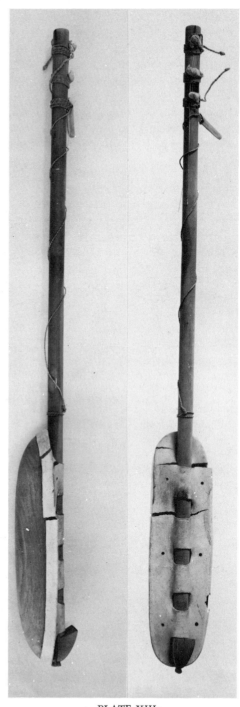

PLATE XIIIa
EGYPTIAN NECKED INSTRUMENT
From the grave of singer Har-Mosé

C. 1500 B.C.

The proportion between length and width of the sound-box was correspondingly smaller and approximated more closely that of the Babylonian instruments. *(Plates III & IV)* The strings varied in number between two and three.

Once in Egypt, these "foreign" instruments became overwhelmingly popular. Many reliefs and paintings on which they have been depicted attest to this, as well as to the Egyptians' love for music and the important role it had in their lives.

In the famous tomb of Nakht, astronomer and scribe, one of the greatest achievements in Egyptian painting has for its subject a trio of charming female musicians. One plays a double flute, the second a harp and the third a necked instrument with carefully marked frets, probably made of gut, wound about the neck. If the measurements between the frets were an accurate reproduction of those on the actual instrument, then it would be possible to reconstruct the musical scale used in Egypt at the time.

PLATE XIIIb
DETAIL

That the performers are female brings to our attention an interesting fact. Before the campaigns of Tuthmosis III in the Near East, only male musicians were observed on reliefs. After the invasion of Syria, female captives of great musical skill were brought to Egypt to entertain the king and his court. From then on Egyptian art included among its subjects female dancers and musicians. Frequently the latter were shown playing the Babylonian necked instruments as well as lyres. *(Plate XIV)* These must have come from the Near East, as lyres were not known in Egypt before this time.

PLATE XIV
COPY OF EGYPTIAN WALL PAINTING FOUND IN A THEBAN TOMB
C. 1420 B.C.

Another relief (1310 B. C. *Plate XV)*, which is now in the Rijksmuseum in Amsterdam, Holland, shows four male musicians — two playing long flutes, a third playing a bow-shaped harp (indicating that this instrument was still in use in its original form), and the fourth playing a necked string instrument to which the plectrum is attached with a cord. They appear to be performing at an offering ceremony at which a priest wearing an animal skin officiates.

The popularity of the Har-Mosĕ instrument is likewise indicated by depictions not only on reliefs and paintings of court entertainment and religious ritual but also on more commonplace objects. A little razor now in the Metropolitan Museum of Art in New York shows a negro servant with a Har-Mosĕ type instrument in his hands. *(Plate XVI)*

Since this and the Babylonian instrument were apparently both widely used in Egypt, it was inevitable that some of their features and characteristics should eventually combine in a later instrument, one which would be the predecessor not only of the guitar but of all necked string instruments, both plucked and bowed. Its proportions came closer to those of the Babylonian prototype; its construction shows the influence of the Har-Mosĕ in-

23

PLATE XV
EGYPTIAN RELIEF FROM THE TOMB OF PATENEMHAB. XVIIITH DYNASTY
C. 1310 B.C.

strument. Its ancestry can thus be traced back to Egypt and Babylonia.

Further developments made this instrument even more similar in form to the guitar. Although no actual instruments have been found to illustrate the changes as they took place, a guitar-like instrument from the Roman period in Egypt, with slight curves along the sides, shows the effects of modification. *(Plate XVIIa)*

Up to this point, the only other instrument with curved sides was the Hittite "guitar" of 1300 B. C. *(Plate VIII)* Perhaps the instrument from the Roman period acquired its curves independently of Hittite influence, but more likely they were the result of Egyptian-Hittite cultural interchange.

It is well-known that these two peoples were in constant contact with each other. After a great battle between the Egyptians and the Hittites, the warring nations signed a peace treaty in 1271 B. C. This was further strengthened when Ramses II of Egypt married the daughter of the Hittite king, Hattushilish III. Thus began a period of trade and friendly relations that opened avenues by which the Hittite "guitar" could have entered Egypt to exert considerable influence on its Egyptian counterpart.

The above-mentioned instrument from the Roman period (c. 30 B. C. — 400 A. D. *Plate XVIIa*), which is now in the Metropolitan Museum of Art in New York, is made entirely of wood. The rawhide soundboard of the past had been replaced with wood on which five groups of small sound holes are visible. (This arrangement of sound holes persisted up to the sixteenth

PLATE XVI
EGYPTIAN BRONZE RAZOR

century A. D. as seen on the Spanish *vihuela*.) (*Plate XXXVI*) The soundbox of the Roman instrument had become smaller in relation to the neck, and, significantly, the beginnings of curves appear at the sides. Four strings attached to pegs piercing the neck signify a reversal of the trend towards reduction of strings. Having reached a minimum of two, the number of strings again increased to four and remained this way for several centuries.

An instrument dated fifth to seventh century A. D. (*Plate XVIIb*), now in the Oriental Institute of Heidelberg, Germany and originally found in a Coptic tomb at Qarara, Egypt, reveals still more changes. The curves along the sides are already quite deep, and the basic guitar shape is apparent, although still at a relatively primitive stage. Most significantly, the back had become completely flat; instead of it curving upward to meet the soundboard, the two surfaces were now attached to each other by strips of wood that form the sides of the soundbox. These features remain to the present day.

This instrument also had four strings, but the upper end of the neck, which widens slightly and carries an interesting design, shows the beginning of a separate tuning box. Unfortunately, the soundboard has been lost, but we can safely assume that it had an arrangement of sound holes similar to that observed on the Roman period instrument. This guitar must have been plucked either with the fingers or with a plectrum, as no bows have as yet been found dating back to this period.

The extent to which the guitar has evolved from its earliest harp-like stages to the period represented by the "Coptic guitar," can be summarized with a quick backward glance over the preceding centuries.

An instrument with horizontal neck, derived from the Sumerian "Queen Shub-Ad's harp", may have been adopted by the Babylonian priesthood. The female captives of Tuthmosis III brought this instrument to Egypt where an instrument, similar in general appearance but different in proportions, had been developed locally. One probably influenced the other, and, in the process, a latter-date ancestor of the guitar evolved. This eventually acquired curved sides, perhaps under the additional influence of the Hittite "guitar". These developments culminated in the "Coptic guitar", after which the history of the guitar became a European phenomenon. Such it was bound to remain for many future centuries.

PLATE XVIIb
EGYPTIAN "GUITAR"
FOUND AT QARARA
C. 5TH CENTURY A.D.
COPTIC PERIOD

PLATE XVIIa

EGYPTIAN GUITAR-LIKE INSTRUMENT
C. 3RD CENTURY A.D. ROMAN PERIOD

CHAPTER *3*

Medieval Europe

*A*ncient Europe had a number of native instruments worthy of historical interest, and a search for them is not as futile as might be supposed. Such instruments are of interest not only in themselves but also because of what they can contribute to our understanding of early European culture in general and, specifically, how they relate to the instruments of our own time. For the purposes of this book, however, we shall confine ourselves to those of the necked string type which are significantly related to the modern guitar.

The first known European string instrument that might have had its origins here dates back to the third century A.D. No actual example has survived but its existence is proved by a depiction on three Roman sarcophagi, of which two are in the Louvre, the other being in the Musei Comunali in Rome. This last is reproduced on *Plate XVIIIa*.

Although some resemblance to the Persian *citar (sehtar)* and the Indian *sarod* may be discerned, it is my feeling that these instruments, which were by then highly developed, were native to Europe. The element of coincidence in similarities between instruments from different parts of the world, each a product of separate regional developments, cannot be totally disregarded.

PLATE XVIIIa
NECKED INSTRUMENT ON ROMAN SARCOPHAGUS
3RD CENTURY A.D.

PLATE XVIIIb
DETAIL OF PULPIT IN SAN LEONARDO AT ARCETRI, FLORENCE
10TH CENTURY A.D.

Examination of the third century instrument shows it to have had a round soundbox which tapers into a wide neck. The sarcophagi in the Louvre show an instrument with as many as ten strings; that which is in the Musei Comunali shows the same instrument with six strings. Here, the musician plucks the strings with his right hand while pressing them against the neck with his left. It should be recalled that all the Near Eastern and Egyptian instruments of approximately the same period previously discussed had four strings or less. Thus, there are no known non-European precedents for these third century instruments, and we can presume their native European origin.

Apparently this type of instrument continued to be in use for many years. A carving of it can still be seen adorning the pulpit of San Leonardo, which was constructed long after the Roman period, in Arcetri, Florence. (*Plate XVIIIb*) The number of strings had decreased to about three but the general form of the instrument on the Roman sarcophagi had been retained with but little change.

Reaffirming the existence of such string instruments in Europe at this early date is documented in a highly sophisticated musical treatise by the Saxon philosopher Boethius (500 A.D.). He describes a one string device or monochord which was used to indicate the pitch of whatever string instruments were played.

It is possible that ensemble playing was practised in Europe then. Vases still exist which are adorned with figures of musicians playing in consort.

Our knowledge of native European necked instruments is further advanced by manuscripts and paintings dating from the ninth century. In Stuttgart, Germany, for instance, there is a famous Psalter dating from the time of the Carolingian Dynasty. On several of its pages are pictures of an extremely interesting "Carolingian" instrument which could be either French or German. (*Plates XIX & XX*) At any rate it is, in all probability, North European since the shape of the soundbox removes it from Moorish or Near Eastern influence.

Another manuscript, the *Commentarius Super Apocalypsum,* was written and illuminated by the scribe Maius in 926 A.D. to illustrate Beatus of Liebana's popular document on the *Revelations of St. John the Divine.* Originally from the Monastery of San Miguel de Escalada (erected in 913 near the city of Leon in northern Spain), this manuscript is now in the Morgan Library of New York. One of the paintings in the manuscript (*Plate XXI*) shows the

PLATE XIXa
PAGE FROM THE "CAROLINGIAN PSALTER"
Representing several musicians. One plays a guitar-like instrument
9TH CENTURY A.D.

PLATE XIXb
PAGE FROM THE "CAROLINGIAN PSALTER"
Representing King David as a shepherd playing a guitar-like instrument
9TH CENTURY A.D.

PLATE XXa
PAGE FROM "CAROLINGIAN PSALTER"
Representing a musician playing a guitar-like instrument
9TH CENTURY A.D.

PLATE XXb
PAGE FROM "CAROLINGIAN PSALTER"
Another representation of a guitar-like instrument
9TH CENTURY A.D.

Lamb of God standing on a medallion, holding a cross and a book. He is adored by twelve of the twenty-four Elders, four of whom play necked instruments of a very large size. These have pear-shaped soundboxes which taper into necks, at the ends of which are perpendicular protrusions containing three tuning pegs, even though the instruments have four strings. Two of the performers pluck these with their fingers. The third uses a plectrum while the fourth appears to be using a sort of bow. (This is one of the earliest representations of the bow in Europe. In another tenth century Beatus manuscript in Madrid *(Plate XXII)*, the bow has already developed considerably.)

A separate painting from the same work shows the Lamb of God on Mt. Zion surrounded by four groups of holy men, all playing necked string instruments. *(Plate XXIII)* These differ from those described above in that the necks are more clearly differentiated from the soundboxes and have a rather more elongated and rectangular shape, although with rounded corners.

These instruments were found not only in Spain but as far north as the Northern Carolingian Empire. Among these, however, only the one represented in the ninth century psalter in Stuttgart developed the shape of the guitar with its characteristic curved sides. This instrument continued in existence through the Middle Ages. It is therefore this ninth century instrument that merits discussion.

The soundbox of the "Carolingian" instrument is rectangular, approximately equal in length to its neck, the upper end of which is a wider, rounded area containing small pegs for the attachment of strings. On some pages these pegs appear to be four in number; on others, five. The strings are of a corresponding number.

These are plucked in two ways: either with a plectrum, as can be seen in most of the illustrations, or with the fingers, as is seen in a picture of King David playing the instrument. Perhaps it would be useful to point out that the biblical David is here portrayed not in an historical context but in a universal role implying no particular location or time. He is shown among his sheep in what appears to be a pastoral setting. The Divine Hand reaches down from the sky and touches David's instrument with one curved finger, possibly to signify that the song of the shepherd was inspired by God. *(Plate XIXb)*

Other pages from the same ninth century psalter show the various uses of this instrument. On one it is being played in consort with a singer and instrumentalists with long, curved horns and a rectangular psaltery or "harp." *(Plate XIXa)* On another, the ensemble is composed of the "Carolingian" instrument and two curved horns. The entertainment is for a monarch, who has his right hand lifted, seemingly in appreciation. *(Plate XXb.)*

PLATE XXI
PAGE FROM THE MANUSCRIPT *Commentarius Super Apocalypsum*
The Lamb of God is surrounded by twelve figures. Four play necked instruments
926 A.D.

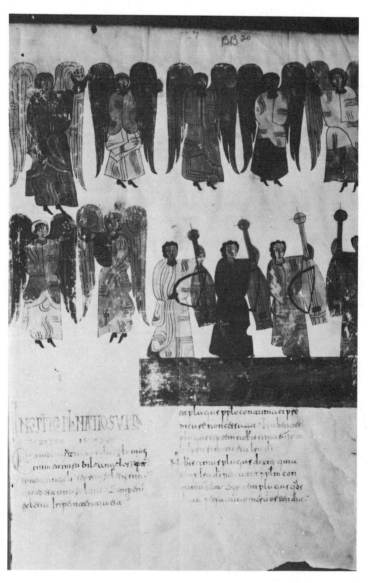

PLATE XXII
PAGE FROM THE MANUSCRIPT *Commentarius Super Apocalypsum*
Four figures play very large instruments with bows
926 A.D.

PLATE XXIII
PAGE FROM THE MANUSCRIPT *Commentarius Super Apocalypsum*
Representing musicians with necked instruments
926 A.D.

PLATE XXIVa
PLASTER CAST OF SCULPTURED ANGELS AT EXETER CATHEDRAL, ENGLAND
14TH CENTURY

The "Carolingian" instrument, therefore, draws our attention to the fact that Europe had a noteworthy indigenous culture, one which attained a high degree of development as exemplified by the *a capella* chanting of Gregorian plainsong. Conversely, such a culture draws our attention to the existence of native European musical instruments of which the "Carolingian" instrument possibly was one.

Evidently the "Carolingian" instrument retained its form up to the fourteenth century. In the Exeter Cathedral in England (mid-fourtenth century), a carved angel, the central figure in a series *(Plate XXIVa),* plays an instrument almost identical to the "Carolingian" model. The similarity extends even to the angle at which the neck meets the soundbox. But at the same time a significant change began to take place so that, eventually, a more advanced instrument began to exist side by side with the "Carolingian" type. This change affected the soundbox of the instrument, its straight sides now giving way to slight curves which became more defined in the course of time.

Representatives of the instrument showing this new development can be found in a number of English cathedrals: Westminster Abbey, Gloucester Cathedral, Chichester Cathedral (where it is shown as a bowed instrument), Tewkesbury Abbey and Beverley Minster, to name a few. Some details on these representations would be relevant.

The vaulting of Tewkesbury Abbey's nave was nearing completion (c. 1128) when the angel-musicians of Exeter were carved. Despite their being contemporary works, however, two of the angels on the magnificent keystones or "bosses" of Tewkesbury's vault held string instruments whose general shapes and proportions are very similiar to the instruments shown in the ninth century psalter and the Exeter Cathedral, but whose sides now show the crucial long and shallow curves. A complete collection of medieval instruments is held by the other angels adorning the vault: bagpipes, an organ, a pipe, tabor, lutina, cymbals and psaltery.

At Lavenham Church, the "guitar" is part of a misericord, a carved wooden projection on the underside of a hinged seat. When this is lifted, the misericord performed the amusing function of providing support to those monks who, though grown tired during lengthy services, still needed to maintain the semblance of standing. Medieval artists took advantage of the hidden position of the misericord by carving on them a menagerie of monsters and other strange creatures. In the Lavenham Church, two human-headed beasts play musical instruments, one the above mentioned "guitar" and the other a bellows with a crutch. *(Plate XXIVb)*

Beverley Minster contains sculptures that (though much restored) still retain their fourteenth century forms. The instrument which interests us also features curves on its sides, but these, instead of being as shallow as those on the Tewkesbury and Gloucester instruments, have been shortened to achieve a shape closer to that of the modern guitar.

PLATE XXIVb
MISERICORD AT LAVENHAM CHURCH. SUFFOLK, ENGLAND
C. 1330

The "Carolingian" instrument of the ninth century had, therefore, obviously undergone a series of changes. Its rectangular soundbox with straight sides had acquired curves. These at first extended almost the entire length of the soundbox, but in time became shorter until the instrument attained a fairly modern guitar shape.

These changes may suggest an independent evolution of the guitar in Europe, but they do not, by any means, constitute the only trend of development, since depictions of guitar-shaped instruments have been found in French and Spanish cathedrals prior to the fourteenth century, specifically in the twelfth and thirteenth centuries.

In tracing the source of these guitars, the Moorish invasion of 711 A. D. comes to mind. It has been frequently cited as being preeminently important in bringing Eastern cultural elements into Europe. Some musicologists have even gone so far as to ascribe to it the introduction of almost all musical instruments into the Western world. The role of the Moors as a cultural force, however, has been overestimated, and sweeping statements on the transplantation of instruments from East to West must be tempered by an awareness of instruments that not only pre-date the Moorish invasion but had, in fact, their origins in Europe.

Having presented the case for the evolution of these native instruments, we now turn to the more definitive course which the guitar followed in its development.

It may be well to start by taking steps in order to avoid ambiguities which could arise as a result of applying the term "lute" to all necked string instruments whose name has not come down to us. Not infrequently we come across statements that confuse guitars with lutes. But these two instruments developed separately, and each has a history of its own.

The word "lute" comes from the Arabic "al-ud" which may be translated as "wood." For our purposes we will use the term "lute" only for those necked, plucked string instruments with a pear-shaped soundbox and a sideless, bowl-like back. We will use the term "guitar" for those necked string instruments which have a flat back and soundbox with curves along the sides.

Like the guitar, the lute may possibly have been native to Europe, but the theory that it was brought by the Moors from Egypt (where representations of it on figurines of the XXIInd Dynasty have been found) must not be too readily dismissed.

Having clarified our use of the terms "lute" and "guitar," we might then examine some of the instruments represented in twelfth and thirteenth centuries French and Spanish cathedrals. As will be seen, these instruments antedated the fourteenth century guitar-shaped instruments which evolved from the "Carolingian" prototype and were at least as highly developed, if not more so. They must, therefore, have had a different lineage, the tracing of which now concerns us.

The Cathedral of Saint-Denis in France is, architecturally, a transition between the Romanesque and Gothic styles. Among the magnificent sculptures on its Royal Portal are those of guitar players whose instruments have a soundbox shaped like a figure 8. They have four semi-lunar sound holes, two on either side of the strings. (*Plate XXV*) If we look back to the Har-Mosĕ instrument, which had six sound holes, and to the Roman period guitar of Egypt, which had five, we can assume that the Saint-Denis instrument represents a gradual decrease in the number of sound holes. This may have been the trend that eventually led to the single rosette of the modern guitar.

The Cathedral of Chartres (thirteenth century), also in France, is an historic landmark — the site of Henry IV's coronation in 1594 and one of the most glorious edifices of its time. On its west facade (1145-1170), there are sculptures that throw some light on musical instruments of this time. Among the figures of the twenty-four Elders that have been carved around the tympanum, one holds a guitar-shaped instrument, also with four sound holes, although these differ in shape from those of the Saint-Denis guitar. It has three strings attached to the same number of pegs. (*Plates XXVI & XXVII.*)

PLATE XXV
DETAIL OF SCULPTURE ON ROYAL PORTAL OF CATHEDRAL AT SAINT-DENIS, FRANCE
12TH CENTURY

A similar instrument turned up one hundred years later in the eastern wing of the Lincoln Cathedral in England. This portion of the edifice was named Angel Choir, after the angels who are shown playing a variety of instruments: pipe and tabor, a trumpet, double pipes, a viol, harp, and the guitar mentioned above. In the midst of the celestial musicians is King David, represented as a winged figure, apparently leading the ensemble.

In Spain, we have an important source of information in the Santiago de Compostela Cathedral, begun in 1078 and finally consecrated in 1211. It was constructed to house the bones of Saint James, allegedly unearthed in Compostela. Of special interest to us is its twelfth century *Portico de la Gloria* or "Gate of Glory" in the west side of the edifice. On this are carved a great variety of instruments played by the ever present twenty-four Elders. *(Plates XXVIII & XXIX)*. Before proceeding with their description, however, it would be helpful to note certain classifications being made at that time.

The French composer and poet Guillaume de Machaut (1304-1377) mentioned "Moorish" and "non-Moorish" guitars in some of his works. There was also a distinction being made between a so-called *Guitarra Morisca* also known as *Guitarra Saracenica* and one called *Guitarra Latina*. The two types were first mentioned by Juan Ruíz of Hita, Spain. The Royal House of Normandy was known to have employed two guitarists, one to play the *Guitarra Latina,* the other to play the *Guitarra Morisca.*

The latter was believed to have been brought by the Moors, hence its name. Its soundbox was oval and it had many sound holes on its soundboard. Since its body had no curves at the sides, it should not be called "guitar" at all.

The *Guitarra Latina,* however, did have curved sides and was thought to have come to Spain from some other European country. It was this type that undoubtedly developed into the modern guitar.

Both types are represented in the "Gate of Glory." The *Guitarra Latina,* several of which are shown *(Plate XXIXb),* is similar in shape to the Saint-Denis and Chartres instru-

PLATE XXVI
DETAIL OF SCULPTURE
CHARTRES CATHEDRAL

ments, but it has two sound holes instead of four such as the French examples have. Apparently, therefore, the *Guitarra Latina* might be further divided into sub-types according to the number of sound holes.

The *Guitarra Morisca,* typically, has an oval body and no curves on the sides. *(Plate XXIXc)* It also has two sound holes in the shape of a figure 8.

It is important to note that the Santiago de Compostela "guitars" were plucked, in contradistinction to the occasional practice of the time of bowing them. These two ways of playing (plucking and bowing) the same kind of instrument lead to the conclusion that the guitar and the viols had a common ancestor. One must, however, guard against the error of calling instruments viols solely on the basis of their being held between the legs and being bowed; an absolute differentiation between the bowed (viol) family and the plucked (guitar) family probably did not materialize until some time later. (It should immediately be recalled that we have used the term "guitar" only in reference to the shape of the instrument.)

I might further point out that regardless of whether the instruments were plucked or bowed, the Spanish designation for necked string instruments was *vihuela.* Thus a vihuela played with the fingers was called *vihuela de mano* or, literally translated,"vihuela of the hand." One plucked with a plectrum was called *vihuela de péndola,* and one that was bowed was called *vihuela de arco* or "vihuela of the bow." At their earliest stages *(Plate XXII)* these instruments were probably structurally identical.

Among the depictions at Santiago de Compostela is one of King David on the so-called Gate of Silversmiths. *(Plate XXX)* He is shown playing a *vihuela de arco.* This proves the existence of this instrument of the rebec type in twelfth century Spain.

Having been confronted with the foregoing list of sculptures and their implications, we are now faced with this question: how to explain the sudden appearance of the guitar in Europe in the twelfth century, a fact indicated by the representations of these instruments in places as far apart as Saint-Denis, Santiago de Compostela and England?

The search for an answer brings us back to Egypt and the Egyptian "guitar." Venice, by virtue of its position as one of Europe's important trading centers, seems a likely port of entry for the Egyptian "guitar." But the more promising alternative is Provence, in Southern France.

Provence has a considerable coastline on the Mediterra-

PLATE XXVII
PLASTER CAST OF FIGURE HOLDING GUITAR-SHAPED INSTRUMENT
DETAIL OF PLATE XXVI

nean, and the trade routes between this area and Egypt were established as far back as the time of the Phoenicians. As has been satisfactorily argued by the critics of the Pirenne thesis, not even the Arab conquest could completely disrupt the trade between Egypt and Southern Europe. It was in the course of this commerce that traders brought the Egyptian "guitar" to Provence. Centuries later representations of it were being featured in sculptures and architectural decor on the continent. In the absence of actual evidence from the seventh to the twelfth centuries in either Egypt or Europe, however, we must consider this explanation hypothetical, although circumstancial evidence favors its statement.

Once in Provence, the guitar encountered those cultural forces which were to carry it throughout France to Spain, Italy and England. These forces were interwoven in the music, literature, history and politics of Europe.

Let us first consider the troubadours of the area, those poet-musicians who composed their own songs and wandered about singing them to all who had the desire and taste to listen. They traveled widely, within and outside of Provence, as far as northern Europe, Italy, England and Spain. They traveled singly, in groups, on their own, or as part of a nobleman's entourage. Some of them served in royal courts for extended periods of time. Thus the troubadour Bernart de Ventadour was in the service of Eleanor of Acquitaine, wife of England's Henry II, an outstanding patron of the arts. In Italy, Peire Vidal served Boniface II, who was Marquis of Montferrat from 1192-1207.

Guillaume IX, Count of Poitiers (1071-1127), was the first known troubadour. The last, as far as can be ascertained, was Guiraut Riquier (1230-1294), who belonged to the court of the brilliant Spanish monarch Alfonso X.

It was customary for the troubadours to sing their songs to instrumental accompaniment. They played a number of instruments, one of which was the guitar. This was favored not only for its musical attributes but also for its portability, a consideration that was important for an itinerant performer.

Taking into account, therefore, the fact that the troubadours covered a vast area in their travels, that they had a wide audience ranging from the masses to the nobility, that they took with them their guitars to accompany their songs, we can readily see the role they must have played in disseminating Provençal culture in general and the guitar

PLATE XXVIII
"GATE OF GLORY." WEST SIDE OF CATHEDRAL OF SANTIAGO DE COMPOSTELA
12TH CENTURY

PLATE XXIXa
DETAIL OF THE "GATE OF GLORY"

PLATE XXIXb

PLATE XXIXc

PLATE XXIXd

DETAILS OF THE "GATE OF GLORY"

in particular.

The popularity achieved by the instrument can be attributed to the nomadic nature of the troubadours. The guitar was as much a part of their appearance as sculptured decorations were in the great cathedrals of Europe. That the dates of these sculptures coincided with the time during which the troubadours were at the height of their fame shows further the relationship between the activity of the troubadours and knowledge of the instrument.

Finally, the absence in Europe of ancestors to an instrument which was already in a high state of development, added to the fact that active trade existed between Provence and Egypt, leads to the conclusion that the guitars used by troubadours were descended directly from the Egyptian "guitar."

This instrument arrived in Spain from Provence by way of Catalonia, then an autonomous province. Previous to its union with Spain in the late Fifteenth century it was culturally closer to Provence than it was to Spain, from which it was separated by mountain ranges. Its language had strong similarities to the Provençal tongue, the *langue d'oc*. The passage of the guitar from Provence to Catalonia was, therefore, natural and virtually inevitable. (We should note here that Catalonia has traditionally been associated with the guitar and its performers. Among others, Fernando Sor and Miguel Llobet were born there.)

Once in Catalonia, the guitar could have crossed to Spain in the hands of itinerant Spanish troubadours. The names of some of these have, fortunately, been recorded.

Jot Aben was a twelfth century troubadour in Spain. Of Arab descent, he was a native of Valencia, on the southern Catalonian border. He is said to have played the guitar (guiterne) and composed songs. The Moorish quality in his music, however, caused him to be exiled, and he became a wanderer, with the guitar as his constant companion. He exemplified the band of men who were responsible for the spread of the guitar in that region.

Juan Nadal was another troubadour whose name and association with the guitar was mentioned in a Valencian document dated 1389.

From the fifteenth century we have Alonso de Carrion, a *jongleur* or "wandering juggler", who frequently accompanied the singing of troubadours unable themselves to play the instrument.

These are but a few of the great numbers of troubadours in medieval Europe whose incessant travels and perform-

PLATE XXX
SCULPTURE OF KING DAVID PLAYING A VIHUELA DE ARCO

ances enriched musical culture in general and gave great impetus to the spread of the guitar on the continent.

From this point on the guitar was increasingly featured in works of art of the Middle Ages. We will satisfy ourselves with a few outstanding examples.

Toward the end of the thirteenth century, the great Spanish king Alfonso X, also known as *el Sabio* or "the Wise", compiled the *Cantigas de Santa Maria,* now recognized as one of the greatest collections of medieval music and literature. Its contents have been studied intently for the insight they give into the history of medieval art. For us, the most interesting aspects of the *Cantigas* are the paintings, which are not only beautiful but also informative. They show musicians playing a variety of instruments. Many kinds of trumpets, horns, harps, bagpipes and percussion instruments are illustrated as well as several types of lutes and guitars. Evidently these two string instruments coexisted in Europe throughout the medieval era and indeed they continued to be played independently of each other until the eighteenth century, when the lute, after a revival in Germany, fell into disuse. It is fortunate that its magnificent literature has not been forgotten.

One of the guitars in the *Cantigas* resembles the guitar of Tewkesbury Abbey and Gloucester Cathedral in England, both of which may represent an indigenous European tradition. We may, therefore, reiterate the possibility of parallel development between the native European instrument and the one transplanted from Egypt and disseminated by the troubadours.

In the ceiling of the church of St. Segundo, in Avila, Spain, there is a fifteenth century painting of a cherub playing a medieval guitar. *(Frontispiece.)* The form of the modern guitar is already recognizable in this example.

From approximately the same period, we have an enameled glass bowl from Venice, an important artistic center at the time and a source of much exquisite glass work. This piece was once in the collection of the Baron Maurice de Rothchild but presently is in the Cleveland Museum of Art.

It is decorated with figures playing musical instruments, three of them stringed. *(Plate XXXI)* Two of these are lute-shaped, although they cannot properly be called lutes since they are bowed. Lutes, it may be recalled, are strictly plucked instruments. The third instrument, however, is clearly a guitar. It has curved sides, well delineated frets, these on a neck that ends in a graceful scroll.

The quantity and the variety of media employed for

this purpose (manuscripts, paintings, sculptures, glass work, etc.) show not only the widespread use of the guitar, but also the lack of standardization in the construction of instruments, the different ways by which they may be played, and the increasing use of the bow for playing the guitar or guitar related instruments. Apparently this was a time of experimentation, hence of development. It was also the time when a completely new branch of musical instruments — the bowed string types — was beginning to gain recognition.

PLATE XXXI
ENAMELED GLASS BOWL FROM VENICE, ITALY
15TH CENTURY

It has often been suggested that the viols and violins developed from the medieval "fiddle" or rebec. But although the idea of bowing may have originated from the same practice on the rebec, this instrument represents something of a dead end in music history. The more plausible theory is that the bowed string instruments evolved from the guitar, and the evidence is clear from the representations previously cited. A few more may be mentioned.

At the National Museum in Prague there is a small painting from the thirteenth century Czechoslovakian manuscript known as the *Master Verborum*. It shows a man bowing a guitar that is almost exactly the same as the ones found in the Chartres and Lincoln Cathedrals.

In the Cathedral of Toledo (fourteenth to fifteenth century), there is a statue of an angel holding an instrument which is a cross between violin and guitar. *(Plate XXXII)*
The neck, tuning head and round sound hole are like those of the guitar. The F-shaped sound holes on either side of the round one, and the curves on the sides of the soundbox are characteristic of the violin. This instrument undoubtedly represents a transition from guitar to violin.

Three other paintings deserve attention. The first, dated 1175, is from a psalter in Glasgow. It portrays David playing a harp, surrounded by a number of musicians with a variety of instruments: a rebec, a psaltery, a hurdy-gurdy, etc. Among them is a bowed guitar, held between the legs of the performer.

The second, an English painting from the thirteenth century, can be found in the British Museum. It is quite an amusing example as it shows animal musicians, among whom is a cat playing a guitar-like instrument with a bow.*

PLATE XXXII
DETAIL OF SCULPTURE
CATHEDRAL OF TOLEDO, SPAIN
14TH-15TH CENTURY

*M. Rickert, *Painting in Britain: The Middle Ages.*

Lastly, there is an early thirteenth century English painting from the famous *Psalter of Robert de Lindsey.* A group of instruments similar to those in the second painting is shown, this time played by men. The guitar is here played with a rather large bow.*

These examples may tend to imply that the practice of bowing the guitar had become more widespread than the practice of plucking it. The sculptures at Compostela, however, must not be forgotten, and we must assume that throughout the medieval era the guitar and the viol were very similar, if not identical, instruments. The evidence that at this time the guitar was both plucked and bowed is overwhelming. Not until the sixteenth century, with the flowering of purely instrumental music, would there be a clear-cut differentiation between bowed and plucked instruments.

Now it is crucially important to emphasize that the lineage which finds the greatest support in the history of the guitar is the one that led from Egypt through Provence to the rest of Europe. The evidence thus far presented points conclusively to the general acceptance of the Egyptian "guitar" as the dominant ancestor of our modern instrument. Its significance is underscored by the probability that it was through its influence that the native European instrument, first seen in the ninth century psalter in Stuttgart, finally adopt the curved sides that made it truly a member of the guitar family.

From this point on the separate line of development, which had been followed by the native European instrument in the early part of its evolution, became incorporated into the mainstream of the guitar's development. The cultural forces that had worked on the native instrument were the same ones that worked on the Egyptian "guitar" and transformed it into a European instrument. From the fusion of the two instruments — the native and the imported one — were born the great families of bowed and plucked musical instruments in Europe. At this stage of its evolution, the guitar moved out of the Middle Ages and onto the threshold of the Renaissance.

*M. Rickert, op. cit.

CHAPTER 4

The Sixteenth Century

Until the Middle Ages, a significant part of the information on the guitar and its lineage has had to be drawn from paintings, sculptures, reliefs, literary works and other art forms which represented or mentioned the instrument and its ancestors. Heavy reliance on indirect evidence is unavoidable — there are few, if any, actual instruments, and documentation is both erratic and scanty.

Beginning with the sixteenth century, however, we find much more direct evidence in the form of instruments that exist to the present day. Literary and historical records have increased, both in number, in accessibility and, perhaps, in reliability. We have sixteenth century guitars from Spain, France and Italy. A *vihuela* from the time of Luys (Luis) Milan *(Plate XXXVI)* is now in the Jacquemart-André Museum in Paris. The so-called Rizzio guitar from France *(Color Plates XLVI a & b)* is in the Royal College of Music in London, and a fine Italian *guitarra battente* dated 1564 *(Color Plate XLIII)* is in the Gemeentemuseum in The Hague. These three examples are among the most significant from this period. They will be discussed in detail later in the book.

Before proceeding with our history, it would be well at this point to consider the etymology of the guitar.

Indications are that the word "guitar" was derived from the Persian word *citar (sehtar)*, which the Persians used as a general term for string instruments. Literally, *tar* means "string" and *ci (seh)* means "three." Citars with more than three strings, however, were quite common. Originally, *tar* also applied to the earliest string instruments from Persia.

PLATE XXXVI
VIHUELA INSCRIBED "MONASTERY OF GUADALUPE"
16TH CENTURY

At present its application has been narrowed down to a particular type of string instrument, an example of which is illustrated on *Color Plate XXXIV*. This instrument, dating from the fourteenth to the sixteenth century, had five strings. The fact that these are single indicate the instrument's age, since more recent *tars* have double strings.

The prefix *ci* was added at a later date and the usage of the term *citar* spread with the expanding sphere of Persian influence.

In 550-530 B.C., the mighty monarch Cyrus the Great extended his empire from the Caucassus in the north to the Indian Ocean in the south. His son Cambyses conquered Egypt in 525 B.C. Not long afterwards the Greeks adopted the word *citar,* altering it into *kithara,* and applied it to an instrument of their own, which bore no resemblance to the Persian instrument, and had no relation to our guitar. The term "guitar" finally evolved, this after modifications in many languages. From a broad usage which embraced a number of types and variants, the meaning of the term has gradually become more exclusive. Finally, it referred specifically to the sixteenth and seventeenth century European guitar.

The close relationship between the original term *citar* and its contemporary derivatives is demonstrated by the following list:

> Sehtar — Persian
> Citar — Persian
> Chitarra — Italian
> Chittara — Italian
> Guiterne — French
> Guiterre — French
> Guittarre — French
> Gitarre — German
> Guitarra — Spanish
> Guitar — English

The course of the guitar's evolution which we have traced in the previous chapter led directly to the development of the four-string and then the five-string guitar. In Spain, however, there occurred a branching off from the main evolutionary stream in the form of another instrument. For some time its course paralleled that of the four- and five-string guitars, but it could not maintain its separate existence. It eventually merged again with the mainstream. This instrument was the *vihuela*.

Originally its name, like citar, was applied to all string

instruments with neck. The earlier guitar literature was that of the *vihuela de mano* and it far exceeded in volume and quality that of the sixteenth century guitar in the rest of Europe. The importance of the *vihuela* is, therefore, evident, and we will discuss it presently, bearing in mind that guitars at an equally high stage of development existed at the same time in Spain and in the rest of Europe.

THE VIHUELA

In the sixteenth century, the originally generic term "vihuela" became limited in popular usage to mean the *vihuela de mano,* which had also changed much in character and appearance since the fourteenth century. The small four-string *guitarra* of the masses had now grown in size and changed its environment to the palaces of the nobility of Spain.

The sixteenth century saw the lute emerge as the favorite instrument of the aristocracy in nearly all of Europe. Spain was a notable exception. In this country the lute had become associated with the Moors and their oppressive rule. Understandably, the Spaniards did not readily take to the instrument. They did, however, appreciate the music that was written for it, hence the search for a means by which the music could be performed on an instrument other than the lute. The aristocrats turned to the popular *guitarra* with its four double strings. They realized that in this instrument, potentially, they had a worthy substitute for the lute.

There were problems to be overcome. A guitar with only four strings did not have resources adequate to meet the requirements of complex, polyphonic music. In addition, the nobles of Spain doubtless were disdainful of the guitar as it was then — an instrument of the common people. To solve these problems, the four-string guitar was enlarged and given six double strings, tuned in the same manner as the present six-string guitar with the exception of the third string, which was tuned a half tone lower. This was the instrument that came to be known simply as *vihuela.* In it, the Spanish aristocracy had an instrument capable of the same sort of polyphonic music being played on the lute. Furthermore, it was distinct from the instrument of the masses.

In its final form, the *vihuela* was a guitar with six double strings made of gut, the same material used by lutenists. Its five sound holes were arranged in a fascinating and revealing manner: they were placed in precisely the same position as those on the Roman period "guitar" from Egypt previously described. *(Plate XVIIa)* This remarkable fact goes far in itself to prove conclusively that the European guitar originated in Egypt.

The large type of *vihuela* was some four inches longer than the modern guitar. The neck had twelve frets, as can be seen by examining the decorations on it, but these no longer are present on the original instrument, having consisted of gut cords and not of metal inlays. *(Plate XXXVI)* The modern guitar also has twelve frets up to the soundbox, and seven successive frets have been added beyond this point.

One of the first *vihuela* players, or *vihuelistas,* whose publications are known to us was Luys (Luis) Milan. This outstanding performer, composer, poet and courtier was born in c. 1500 of aristocratic Valencian parents. In *El Cortesano,* Milan's last work, published in 1561, he gave an account of life in the Valencian court, and asserted that among the pursuits all courtiers must follow, the art of music is an important one.

In 1535 he published a book, *Libro de Musica de Vihuela de Mano Intitulado "El Maestro",* which he dedicated to King John III of Portugal, his admirer and benefactor, who provided him with an annual pension. This was probably Milan's most important work. (The cover of the original copy is interesting for its picture of Orpheus serenading birds and other animals with his *vihuela.) (Plate XXXIX b)* An interesting passage from the book deals with the tuning of the *vihuela:*

"If the *vihuela* is big, use the first string that is thicker than thin. And if the *vihuela* is small, have the first string thinner than thick. After doing this, raise [tune] the first string as high as it will go and after that you will tune the other strings to the tuning point of the first as will be later taught to you."

Since Milan says that the first string should be tuned "as high as it will go," we can be sure that there was nothing at this time resembling absolute pitch. In addition, the frequent statements one hears to the effect that the *vihuela* had its top string tuned to G must be considered as applying only to *vihuelas* of a very small size. A gut string on a larger instrument, if tuned this high, would break in practically no time. The technique of tuning simply involved tuning the highest string to whatever pitch it could hold and then tuning the other strings according to the pattern of fourths, with a major third between the third and fourth strings.

Milan also enlightens us on the method of determining the quality of the strings to be selected:

"The *vihuela* should be set with strings that are good and not false. And to know if the string is not false you have to do the following: You will stretch with two fingers of each hand the string which should be exactly as long as needed. After the string is thus stretched, you will touch it with another finger as if you want to play it and if the string vibrates as if they are two strings, it is good; and if it vibrates as if it is more than two strings then it is not good and it should not be used on the *vihuela*."

Although the modern guitar no longer has double strings, modern guitarists would undoubtedly spare themselves much needless frustration if they followed Milan's simple advice, because even in this advanced age of technology, many false strings are produced as all guitarists are woefully aware!

The earliest known surviving *vihuela* is at present in the Jacquemart-André Museum in Paris. *(Plate XXXVI)* The instrument unquestionably dates from the sixteenth century. It displays the basic features already described; that is it had five sound holes arranged in the usual manner of the *vihuela* of that time and it once had twelve gut frets on the neck. The curves at the sides of the soundbox are relatively shallow and the soundbox is considerably longer than the neck of the instrument. In this respect it differs from the proportions of the modern guitar, the neck and soundbox of which are approximately equal in length.

The high degree of the *vihuela's* development may be deduced from the musical and technical complexity of the literature written for it and published by Luys Milan in 1535. From this it may be assumed that the *vihuela* of the nobility began to develop at least a century prior to this date. It survived until the eighteenth century in Spain and Portugal as the following examples will demonstrate.

A fine seventeenth century example *(Color Plates XXXV a & b)* comes from Portugal. Beautifully ornamented and more advanced structurally than the sixteenth century *vihuela* described above, it has six double strings and its proportions and single sound hole design are identical to those of the regular five-string guitar.

The last known *vihuela* is dated 1700 and represents the instrument's final stages of development. *(Plate XXXVII)* The workmanship is not comparable to that of the French

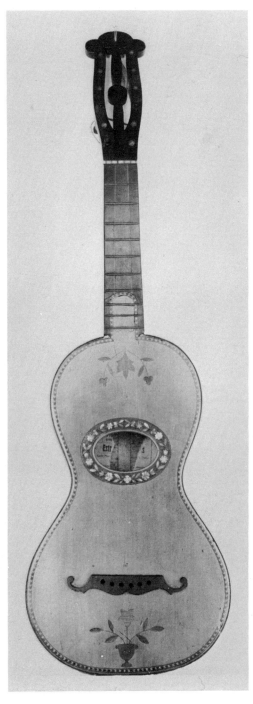

PLATE XXXVII
VIHUELA
C. 1700

and Italian luthiers of the same period, but the instrument itself is interesting for its features. Its frets are metal, the curves along the sides have deepened, and the single sound hole is of an unusual oval type.

The popularity of the instrument is evident from the large quantity of music still extant written for it. It follows that the construction of *vihuelas* must have been a flourishing business, but the name of only one constructor of *vihuelas* has come down to us. Bermudo, in his *Libro de la Declaración de Instrumentos Músicos* (1555), mentions only his first name: Diego.

Music for the *vihuela* was written in notation known as *tablature*, a system which differs markedly from modern notation. A page from Miguel de Fuenllana's *Orphenica Lyra, 1554 (Plate XXXVIII)* will serve as an illustration. Although this music was composed for four and five-string guitars, the principle involved in its writing is the same as that used in *vihuela* tablature.

Each line of the staff represents a string of the instrument. (All six lines would be used in music for the *vihuela*.) In Spanish and Italian tablatures, the top string is represented by the bottom line, while in French and English tablatures, the reverse would be the case. Only Luys Milan, among the Spanish *vihuelistas*, used the latter system. The numbers on the lines indicate the fret to be stopped on that particular string. A zero (0) stands for an open string, the number one (1) for the first fret, the number two (2) for the second fret, and so forth. In contrast, English and French guitar and lute tablatures used letters instead of numbers: "a" for an open string, "b" for the first fret, etc.

Note values are indicated by various note types placed above the staff. These are similar to our present day notes, sometimes differing only in their diamond-shaped noteheads.

To illustrate this system, here is a short passage from Fuenllana's *vihuela* music, first in tablature and then transcribed into modern notation:

PLATE XXXVIII
PAGE OF TABLATURE FOR FOUR AND FIVE STRING GUITARS FROM *Orphenica Lyra*

To our knowledge, the first book of Spanish tablature for the *vihuela* was Luys Milan's *"El Maestro",* published in Valencia in 1535. It contains six Spanish *villancicos,* six Portuguese pieces in the same form, six Italian *sonettos,* no less than forty *fantasias,* four *tientos,* and six *pavanas.* It is deplorable that this music, great as it is, is heard so infrequently.

The purpose of *El Maestro* was essentially pedagogical, and Milan's theories, since they are still applicable today, would be worth quoting:

> "The intention of this book is to show the music of the hand *vihuela* to a beginner who has never played in the order with which the teacher instructs a pupil . . . . Because, if from the start the teacher gives music that is difficult to someone who has never played, he will lose interest and will think that everything is difficult. And giving to beginners easy music will make them feel happy with what they do, and everything will appear easy to them. And the truth is, that most things are easy when a person can do them, unless he makes them difficult when he does not want to learn."

In less than three years another important volume of *vihuela* music appeared. This was *Los Seis Libros del Delphin de Musica* by Luys de Narvaez, native of Granada and court *vihuelista* to King Philip II. He was reputed to be a remarkable performer, capable of improvising polyphonically in four voices. His book, published in Valladolid in 1538, contains the first known themes with *diferencias* or variations. Narvaez' themes included the well-known ballads *Conde Claros* and *Guárdame las Vacas* ("Guard the Cows For Me"). The latter was so immensely liked that Valderrabano wrote one hundred twenty variations on it, Pisador wrote thirty-seven, Mudarra twelve and Venegas de Henestrosa five.

Following the *Delphin de Musica* was the *Tres Libros de Musica en Cifra para Vihuela* by Alonso de Mudarra, published in Seville in 1546 when Mudarra was a canon at the Seville Church. Having traveled to Italy, the composer learned Italian, the language he used for the texts of some of his songs.

This collection of tablatures contains the finest instrumental compositions of the Renaissance. In one of his *fantasías,* Mudarra imitates the harp playing of the celebrated virtuoso Ludovico. This composition carries two interesting and charming comments by the composer. At the beginning he says that the piece is "difficult until understood," and just before the chromatic closing section he says that "from here until just before the end there are some false notes, but when played well they do not sound bad."

The next book of tablatures for *vihuela* was entitled *Silva de Sirinas,* written by Enrique de Valderrabano and published in Valladolid in 1547. It includes a piece for two *vihuelas* and several compositions by Juan Vázquez, conductor of the choir at Burgos Cathedral during the early part of the sixteenth century. A copy of this book in the Nationalbibliotek in Vienna ends with three handwritten pages.

The folk element in music was not overlooked by the composers of the time. In 1552, the first book of *vihuela* music utilizing folk melodies was published in Salamanca under the name *Libro de Musica de Vihuela.* It was written by Diego Pisador and included a *villanesca* (song with several voices) entitled *La Cortesía,* which was actually a parody of the stately *pavanas* of the nobles.

Shortly after the publication of Pisador's book, one of the most outstanding works of the sixteenth century, *Orphenica Lyra* by Miguel de Fuenllana, was published. It was dedicated to Infante Don Philip. *(See Plate XL and dust jacket of this book.)*

Fuenllana was one of the most accomplished performers on the *vihuela,* despite his congenital blindness. He was in the employ of the Marquesa de Tarifa.

Orphenica Lyra contains a total of one hundred seventy-four pieces arranged in six volumes. These consist of religious and secular music by a wide variety of composers. They were written for the regular *vihuela* of six double strings, as well as for the five double string *guitarra.* Also included were fifty-five *fantasías* and *tientos* for two, three, and four voices. The last of the six volumes contains several compositions for the four double string guitar. The voice parts of Fuenllana's songs were printed in red ink and there has been much controversy as to whether or not the *vihuela* player is supposed to play this line.

The last known publication of music for the *vihuela* was *El Parnaso* by Esteban Daza, published in 1576 in Cordoba. It contains *fantasías,* motet transcriptions, *romanzas* and *villanescas* in the Castilian dialect.

In addition to the books of music specifically intended for *vihuela,* others were written by three important organists of the sixteenth century with indications that their compositions could be played on the *vihuela* as well as on the organ. The greatest of these organist-composers was

Antonio de Cabezón, who became known as the "Spanish Bach." Like Fuenllana, he was blind from birth (1510). He was a native of Burgos and his music was published twenty-two years after his death in Madrid in 1578. The title of his book *Obras de Música para Tecla y Harpa y Vihuela* indicates that the music could be performed on either one of these instruments — the keyboard, the harp, or the *vihuela.*

The second of this group was the Dominican monk Fray Tomás de Santa María, a pupil of Cabezón. His book *Arte de Taner Fantasía assi Tecla como Vihuela* was published in Valladolid in 1565.

Luys Venegas de Henestrosa was the third of these organists who used the *vihuela* as an alternate instrument. His book *Libro Nuevo para Tecla, Harpa y Vihuela* was published in 1557. In it he introduced a tablature system that uses the first seven Arabic numerals for the seven notes of the scale.

Books dealing with the *vihuela* were also written in Portugal. We might cite the *Arte Nueva para Tecla y Vihuela* by Mateo dè Aranda, who also composed for the instrument. He was a chamber musician at the Cathedral of Lisbon in 1533. Eleven years later he became professor of music at the University of Coimbra.

Thus we see the richness and variety of the *vihuela* repertoire. It began to blossom in fourteenth century Spain and flourished in the highly favorable atmosphere of the sixteenth century golden age of Spanish music. This was the time of the great masters Victoria and Morales, whose supremacy lay in the field of choral music; of Cabezón and Cabanilles, keyboard composers; of Diego Ortiz, whose specialty was music for the viols. The *vihuelistas* contributed their share to the glory that was Spanish culture during that century. For this they deserve a prominent place in the history of that country's music and in the history of instruments which gave impetus to the growth of the literature for modern guitar.

THE FOUR-STRING GUITAR

We have already noted that the four-string Egyptian "guitar," once arrived in Europe, underwent a considerable change in form. The number of its strings became variable, medieval art giving us evidence of three, four, and five-string types. We are reminded of the examples from Santiago de Compostela Cathedral: one instrument has four strings, the others have three. One of the sculptures from the Saint-Denis Cathedral shows a four or possibly a five-string type. The sculptures at Lincoln Cathedral included a four-string plucked guitar and a five-string bowed instrument of a very similar form. Perhaps the five-string types were influenced by the native European instrument, the first illustration of which was seen in the ninth century psalter and which reappeared at Exeter Cathedral, still in its five-string form.

Out of these varieties, however, the four-string guitar emerged as the most popular by the end of the medieval period. All of its four strings were double in most of Europe with the exception of Italy, where the first string remained single. Correspondingly, the tuning of the Italian instrument differed from the standard system. Whereas the general practice was to tune the lowest course in octave, with the remaining three each tuned in unison, the Italians tuned the two lowest courses in octave, the remaining double course in unison, the first string (cantino) being single. Both systems used the tuning G, C, E, A most frequently, the same as the first four strings on the modern guitar. This, eventually, became the standard manner, the lower tunings being used for the larger instruments.

In Spain, there appeared to have been two main tuning systems for the four-string guitar. These were mentioned by the monk Juan Bermudo in his work of 1555, *Declaración de Instrumentos*. He called one *a los viejos* (in the old style) and the other, *a los nuevos* (in the new style). The first tuning was G-D-F♯-B as on the modern guitar except for the lowest string, which was a tone lower. This tuning, according to Bermudo, was "more suitable for old ballads and 'musica golpeada' (strummed music) than for music of the present time." The "new tuning" is identical to the tuning of the first four strings of the modern guitar.

It is ironic that while, originally, court musicians had considered it beneath their dignity to play on the "vulgar" guitar, they later seem to have applied the newly developed sophisticated technique of the *vihuela* to the instrument which had been its model.

The first of the Spanish tablatures to include serious music for the four-string guitar were those of Alonso Mudarra, published in 1546 in Seville. There are six pieces for this instrument in the book: four *fantasías,* a *pavana* and the ubiquitous *romanesca,* "Guárdame las Vacas." The first *fantasía* is the only published piece in the "old tuning;" the rest of the pieces are in the "new tuning."

The second work to include four-string guitar music was Miguel de Fuenllana's *Orphenica Lyra.* Besides a *villancico* by the Burgos choirmaster Juan Vázquez, there are several *fantasías* and a "Crucifixus" setting by Fuenllana himself.

(Plate XXXVIII.) Since these are all in the "new tuning," they may be performed directly on the first four strings of the modern guitar.

The last known work containing music for this instrument was Juan Carlos Amat's *Guitarra Española y Vandola de Cinco Ordenes y de Quatro,* published in Barcelona in 1586. *(Plate XXXIXa)* Second and third printings were made in Lérida in 1627, and in Valencia in 1639. This volume is important since it is the first known method for the five-string guitar, even though it includes music for the four-string instrument. This, however, was intended for the Italian system involving three double strings and one single, rather than for the Spanish, which called for four double strings. A close relationship with Italy is thus indicated here.

As these three Spanish tablatures were being published, the popularity of the four-string guitar was rising in France and Italy. In the latter country it had begun in the fifteenth century when a guitarist by the name of Janni was employed, in 1463, by one of the most powerful Italian families, the Sforzas of Milan, who were well-known patrons of the arts. For them, da Vinci designed a fabulous monument which unfortunately was never executed.

Not too long afterwards, music publishing was revolutionized when Ottavio Petrucci (1466-1539) set up the first movable type press for the printing of music. This event was an integral part of the cultural golden age in Italy known as the Renaissance — the age which saw great creations in painting, sculpture and architecture, the age of geniuses such as Michelangelo (1475-1564) and Leonardo da Vinci (1452-1519). The latter, incidentally, was an outstanding virtuoso on the lyre. He possessed an intimate knowledge of music and his biographer, Vasari, claimed that "he surpassed all other musicians."

Petrucci published his first tablature book in 1507. This set the stage for the appearance of many such works throughout the century.

A collection of guitar music was published in Venice under the title *Libro de tabolatura de chitarra.* It was composed by Paolo Virchi (d. c. 1610), famous guitarist and organist at the courts of Modena, Ferrara and Mantua. The many cases of organists who were also guitarists lead us to believe that the guitar was more highly respected in Italy than is usually admitted.

The growing number of music publications was paralleled by the number of noted guitar players. Several of these were mentioned by Scipione Cerreto in his book, *Della Practica Musica Vocale e Strumentale,* published in

Naples in 1601. A few of these names are cited below.

Fabio Caltelano was described as an excellent performer on the *chitarra* of seven strings (i. e., three double and one single).

Filippo Carafa played both guitar and lute. This fact is quite revealing, as a lutenist of that time would hardly stoop to play the guitar if it had no respectable repertoire. The assumption that sixteenth century Italians only strummed their guitars may therefore be disregarded as dubious.

Antonio Miscia from Naples is described, like Castelano, as an excellent performer on the four-string guitar.

In France, the effects of music printing became manifest. The most influential publishing house was established in Paris by the famous Adrian Le Roy (d. 1599) and his partner and brother-in-law, Robert Ballard. From 1551 to 1555, five books of guitar tablature were issued. Although the music in these collections does not in general compare with that of the contemporary Spanish *vihuela* school, it, nevertheless, has a high degree of sophistication.

The first and third books contain *fantasías* and pieces in dance form, such as *branles, galliards,* etc. The second book, consisting of music for voice and guitar, reveals instrumental writing sufficiently involved to bear comparison with the music of the *vihuelistas.* All of these compositions in the first three books, with the exception of only three pieces, were written by Le Roy himself. The fourth book contains *fantasies, psalms, chansons* and a composition entitled *La Guerre,* written to commemorate the capture of Crown Prince "Johann Friedrich von Sachsen" at the battle of Mulberg. The contents of this book were composed by M. Gregoire Brayssing of Augsburg, Bavaria. The fifth book is a collection of compositions by Le Roy, Bonard, Arcadet, Certon and De Bussy.

That these French publications included compositions of so many masters is sufficient proof that a true school of guitar playing existed in France in the sixteenth century, and that the resources of the four-string guitar, for which the works were written, were adequate to meet the variety of effects required. A study of the music reveals this aspect of technique: that only the thumb and the first and second fingers of the right hand were used to pluck the strings, the third finger apparently being considered unnecessary.

The following French publications are worth mentioning: *Tablature de Guiterne,* printed in 1550 by Guillaume Morlaye, French composer, "lutenist and citizen of Paris," publisher of his own music as well as that of his teacher

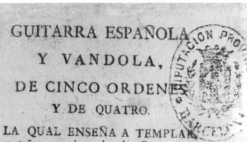

PLATE XXXIXa
COVER OF *Guitarra Espanola y Vandola*
BY JUAN CARLOS AMAT

PLATE XXXIXb
COVER OF *El Maestro*
BY LUYS MILAN

Albert de Ripe. The publications of the latter, over a period of ten years, was made possible by a grant from the king in 1552, given to Morlaye for this specific purpose. To accomplish this task, Morlaye formed a partnership with publisher Michael Fezandant.

Manière de bien et justement entoucher les lucs et guiternes, published in 1556 by Jacques Pelletier of Mans.

Lucs et guiternes by Elie Vinet (1519-1587), a work similar to Pelletier's, issued in 1557 in Poitiers.

Tablature de guiterne by Simon Gorlier, the third in a series of four books, published between 1558 and 1560. Gorlier was his own printer.

Instruction pour apprendre la tablature de guiterne, a method book by Jean Antoine de Baif, poet, musician and guitarist who was born in Venice in 1532 and died in Paris in 1589.

From Germany, we have the names of two guitar players. One is Michael Janusch, who is said to have written a piece for flute and guitar in the sixteenth century. This work stands out as the only composition for this instrumental combination at this early date. The other guitar player was Michel Mulich, "chitarrist" in the Dresden Hoff Kapelle in 1590.

This formidable list of Italian, French and German guitarists and composers, and the depictions of the four-string guitar in works of art such as the Venetian glass bowl previously mentioned *(Plate XXXI),* attest not only to the popularity that had been gained by the instrument but also to the fact that it had entrenched itself firmly in the musical life of these countries. Even the list of guitarists we have given must represent only a very small percentage of those who lived in the sixteenth century. There were undoubtedly a great many more who must remain forever anonymous, whose music never reached the press (as it was nearly impossible to publish without royal sanction), and whose manuscripts have been irredeemably lost.

From the fifteenth century on guitarists were to become a part of many an aristocratic retinue. During this period, and later, in the sixteenth century, the invention of the printing press brought about revolutionary changes. These changes stimulated further development of the instrument and its music, fusing and crystalizing until, finally, the foundation was firm enough to support the remarkable expansion that was to take place in the seventeenth century.

FIVE-STRING GUITAR

We have noted the co-existence of three, four, and five-

PLATE XL
COVER OF *Orphenica Lyra* BY MIGUEL DE FUENLLANA

string guitars in the Middle Ages. By the fifteenth century the four-string instrument – i.e. four double-strings – excelled over the other types in popularity. In the sixteenth century it in turn was gradually replaced by the five double string guitar.*

The first known evidence of a true five-string guitar (as distinguished from the early five-string types seen in English cathedrals) is an interesting Italian engraving *(Plate XLI)* by Marc Antonio Raimondi (1480-1530). Its subject is Giovanni Philotheo Achillini (1466-1513), poet, philologist, jurist, theologian and musician — clearly a worthy aspirant towards the Renaissance ideal of the well-rounded man. The date of this engraving is essential to our history because it indicates the earliest possible date at which the five-string guitar became known.

The face of the poet-musician has been so carefully captured that Achillini must personally have posed for the artist. Obviously, he must have done so before his death in 1513, sometime between the last decade of the fifteenth century and the first decade of the sixteenth. This deduction is corroborated by authorities on graphic art, who place this work in Raimondi's early period, roughly, the last decade of the fifteenth century. If this is the case then the guitar shown in the engraving must have originated long before the engraving — at least two or three decades earlier. We can, therefore, safely place the origin of the five-string guitar in Italy in the fifteenth century.

The engraving shows Achillini in a beautiful and carefully detailed landscape. Behind him is a group of gnarled trees, from the top of which projects a pole that holds a plaque with the name "Philoteo" marked on it. The poet uses his guitar case as a footstool, but he places his right foot on it instead of the left, as in modern practice. The guitar he holds must have had five double-strings, a deduction which may be made from the number of tuning pegs; there are five of these on each side of the tuning head. The Renaissance being a period during which faithful reproduction was expected in art, we can accept the accuracy of this number. The instrument itself is at least as large as its modern counterpart. Indeed, the soundbox appears to be longer than that of the present day guitar.

The thumb of Philotheo's left hand protrudes above the neck, a position for which he would have been severely criticized had he had a modern teacher.

It must be emphasized that the high level of development apparent on this guitar proves that Achillini's instru-

*From this point on, references to the four or five-string guitar will imply four or five double strings unless otherwise specified.

PLATE XLI
PORTRAIT OF GIOVANNI PHILOTHEO ACHILLINI BY MARC ANTONIO RAIMONDI

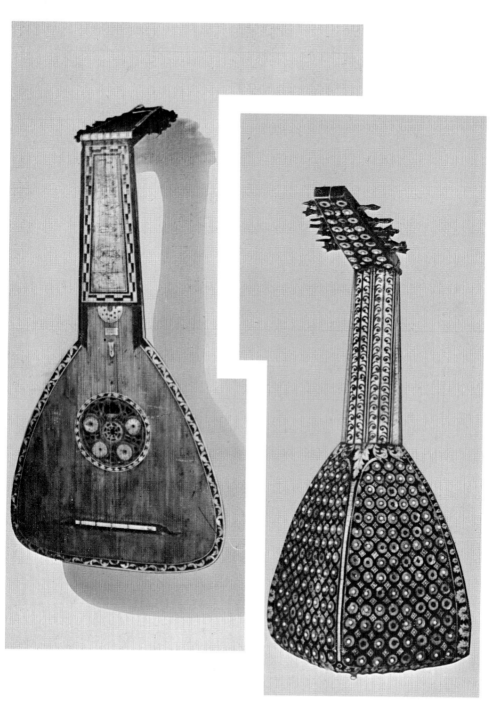

PLATE XLIIa
VENETIAN LUTE-LIKE INSTRUMENT WITH SEVEN DOUBLE STRINGS

Cf. p. 73

PLATE XLIIb
DETAIL OF PLATE XLIIa

Cf. p. 73

ment could not have been a "young" instrument.

Its fine construction draws our attention to the excellent craftsmanship for which Italian luthiers of this period were known. An example of their skill and artistry is given on *Color Plate XLII a & b,* which illustrates an unusual lute-like instrument viewed from three different angles. The original instrument is now in the collection of V. M. Eitingon of New York. The exquisite ivory decoration on the back, and the etchings of scenes drawn from knighthood and chivalry which adorn the neck, are more eloquent than any words could describe.

Most of these craftsmen have become anonymous with time. One of the few who escaped oblivion was a Florentine named Capiari, maker of various types of string instruments including the guitar.

Once the capabilities of the five-string guitar were realized in Italy, it gradually gained prominence. Many paintings and other works of art show it being played alone or in ensemble with other instruments or singers. One engraving by Gaspare Osello, dated 1563, shows Apollo, god of Music, with nine muses on Mount Parnassus, traditional home of the arts. The work was based on a drawing by Luca Penni; hence, the original depiction dates still earlier.

The subject matter is typical of Renaissance humanism in its involvement with Greek Classicism. At the same time, the viola d'amore which Apollo is shown playing, gives the picture a touch of contemporaneity; it was an instrument of Penni's and Osello's time. Below Apollo and to his left are five of the muses, one of whom sings from a book of music. The others play an instrument each: a lute, a small positif organ, a long trumpet, and a pair of cymbals. On the other side of the picture are the remaining four muses, one playing a viola da gamba, two providing percussion accompaniment with a tambourine and a triangle, and another playing a guitar, the sides of which are curved much in the same way as are the sides of the violin. In contrast to the strange hand position of Achillini in the previously described engraving, this muse holds her finger perpendicular to the strings, thus conforming more closely to modern technique. The amazing variety of instruments being played together indicates a rich instrumental tradition in Italian music, and it is gratifying to see that the guitar is presented on an equal footing with such distinguished "colleagues" as the viola da gamba and the viola d'amore.

The first actual Italian guitar of which I have knowledge is dated 1564. *(Color Plate XLIII)* Its maker is unknown to us. That the date is clearly marked (at the base of the

beautifully inlaid portion of the neck) is unusual among sixteenth century guitars, but it is extremely helpful because
it provides us a basis for comparison with other guitars
whose dates and origins are doubtful.

The soundboard of this instrument is decorated with inlays of mother-of-pearl, the finger-board and tuning head
with ivory and black foliage designs. Its five double strings
do not terminate at the bridge but pass over it, being then
fastened at the very bottom of the soundbox. This feature,
as well as similar designs around the sound hole, and an
identical tuning head shape, can be seen on another guitar
which is now in the Boston Museum of Fine Arts. *(Plate
XLIV)* This instrument, therefore, dates to the sixteenth
century and may even be the work of the same luthier.
Both instruments show a technique of construction undoubtedly used throughout this century.

The five-string guitar had a derivative known as the
guitarra battente. It is characterized by a soundbox the back
of which curves gently outwards instead of being simply
flat. An example of this type of guitar, also from the
sixteenth century, is shown on *Color Plate XLV*. It has a
bridge with foliage designs curving backwards from each
end. This motif was to become very popular later on. The
back of the neck is adorned with black interweaving
branches and volutes on a white background, a pattern used
also on the necks of many lutes of this period. (One illustration comes from the cover of Fuenllana's *Orphenica Lyra*
shown on *Plate XL.*) The back of the soundbox is decorated with simple white stripes.

In its earlier days, the *guitarra battente* was primarily
a strummed instrument, hence its name, *battente,* from the
Italian word *battere,* "to strike." By the beginning of the
sixteenth century, however, the *battente* became a plucked,
in addition to being a strummed, instrument. Works by
composers such as Caliginoso and Granata give evidence
of this development. Some of these compositions require
both plucking and strumming within one piece; others call
for plucking exclusively. It is therefore obvious that in this
period both the *battente* and the flat-backed guitar were
plucked as well as strummed.

A question might now arise as to why the backs of the
battente guitars were slightly curved. Three possible reasons, one complementing the other, may be suggested.
First, the guitar makers of this time may have wanted to
imitate to some extent the curved back of the lute while
still maintaining the identity of the guitar. In determining

PLATE XLIII
GUITARRA BATTENTE. ITALIAN SCHOOL
1564

Cf. p. 73

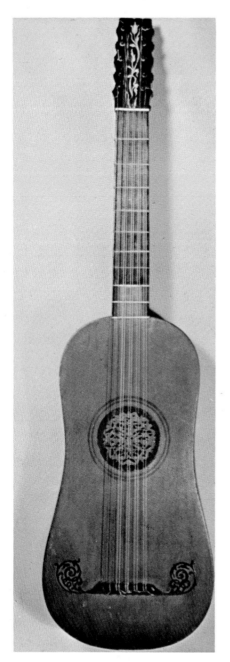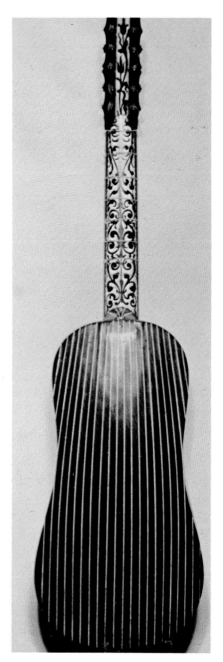

PLATE XLV
GUITARRA BATTENTE. ITALIAN SCHOOL
16TH CENTURY

Cf. p. 74

PLATE XLIV
GUITARRA BATTENTE. ITALIAN SCHOOL
16TH CENTURY

the depth of the curve that the back of the guitar could take, they were of course bound by the curved sides of its soundbox, its main distinction from the lute.

Secondly, there may have been an attempt to increase the volume of sound produced by the guitar. This, apparently, was being diminished by the intricate carvings that virtually covered the rosettes or sound holes of the guitars. The sixteenth century craftsmen felt that by slightly curving the back, they could solve the problem of limited sound without sacrificing the ornate designs on the rosettes.

Lastly, it is possible that the curve on the back of the *guitarra battente* was favored because it allowed for more elaborate ornamentation and fluting.

The popularity of the *guitarra battente* is attested to by its frequent representation in paintings. Two outstanding instances should be cited.

One is entitled *Suonatore di chitarrone* (1590) by an imitator of Caravaggio. This painting is now in the Pinacoteca, Turin. It shows a suave and gentlemanly musician playing a *chitarrone,* a type of large bass lute, which he leans on the table in front of him. Also on the table are an open book of music, a tambourine and a *guitarra battente.* Since the *chitarrone* and tambourine were used primarily for accompaniment, this picture suggests that the *battente* could not have been performing the same function; rather, it was being used as a solo instrument in the performance of polyphonic music.

The other painting is *Il Concerto* by Leonello Spada (1576-1622). Although the work is dated 1615, it is certainly indicative of musical practices that were in vogue not only at that time but many years before. It shows a group of three musicians who appear to be in conversation with each other. The central figure is probably a guitarist, an assumption we can make from the *guitarra battente* on the table before him. His companions are a lutenist and a violinist. To the right of the painting, a little boy holds another violin and shyly suggests, his index finger on his smiling mouth, that the audience should refrain from interrupting the discussion. This picture seems to indicate that the *guitarra battente* was equal to the violin and the lute. As such, it must have enjoyed considerable prestige.

The many depictions of the five-string guitar and its derivative, the *guitarra battente,* also reveal the Italian flair for elegant and lavish decoration, and the special care taken to apply this to their instruments. This same love for ornamentation inspired the remarkable creations in metal and jewelry by Benvenuto Cellini (1500-1571), whose father, incidentally, was a maker of musical instruments and a musician himself. It was likely that he and the luthiers of his time influenced each other to some extent.

The same observation on the taste for decoration probably holds true for the French if one instrument in particular — the famous Rizzio guitar — can be considered an indication. Its story is a rather interesting one, and since it is closely connected with certain events in the life of Mary Queen of Scots, we might briefly follow the life of this unfortunate woman.

Born in 1542, Mary was betrothed at the age of five to the dauphin, Francis, son of the French king, Henri II. The royal couple were eventually married in 1558 when Mary was sixteen. In 1559, they became King and Queen of France. Francis died toward the end of the year 1560. A year later the widowed queen returned to her native Scotland. In the same year she hired as court musician a bass singer from Turin by the name of David Rizzio, who had come to Scotland as a member of the Piedmontese ambassador's entourage. Mary was so pleased with Rizzio that, in 1564, she made him her private secretary. He retained his post until 1566,when he was stabbed to death by several nobles who suspected him of being the Queen's lover.

During his years of service to the Queen, Mary gave Rizzio a magnificent guitar as a present. This came to be known as the Rizzio guitar. *(Color plate XLVI a & b)* It was part of a large collection of many different instruments that Mary, who was a very capable musician, had brought along with her household effects from France to Scotland. There can be no doubt that this guitar was made especially for Mary and was presented to her when she was Queen of France. This is amply demonstrated by the extraordinary workmanship of the instrument and the extravagant use of the emblem of French royalty, the *fleur de lys,* around the rosette and on the tuning pegs. These facts allow us to date the instrument between 1559 and 1561, the time of Mary's reign.

The Rizzio guitar is superbly decorated with tortoise shell, ivory, mother-of-pearl and ebony. The rosette is three-dimensional, carved with incredible intricacy and grace. It is surrounded by sixteen delicate *fleur de lys* executed in mother-of-pearl. The same motif reappears on the ten tuning pegs, all of which are carved in this form. On the back of the neck is a series of ivory chevrons inlaid with ebony.

I could not resist showing my photographs of the Rizzio guitar to a well-known guitar maker and close friend of mine. He stated that it would require a year just to construct a similarly decorated neck, let alone the rest of the instrument!

If the Rizzio guitar can be taken as an indication, guitar-making in sixteenth century France was a highly sophisticated craft. Perhaps it was the exclusiveness of the profession that accounts for the fact that the names of only a few guitar makers have come down to us. One was Philippe Flac, whose workshop was in Lyon from 1568 to 1572. Another was Colson, actually a father-and-son team from Mirecourt, the son, apparently, the better craftsman of the two.

It would have been of great interest to add to these French and Italian examples at least a few from Spain. Unfortunately, however, no actual instrument of this period has survived from that country. Perhaps the great popularity of the six-string *vihuela* overshadowed the five-string guitar. Nevertheless, we know of its existence from the writings of Spanish authors and musicians.

Miguel de Fuenllana, one of the greatest *vihuelistas* who wrote for the four-string guitar, also included music for the five-string type in his publication of 1554, *Orphenica Lyra.* There is a total of nine pieces for the latter instrument: two excerpts from a mass for the Virgin Mary by Morales, an outstanding composer of choral music at the time of Fuenllana, a setting of a *villancicode* by Vásquez, and six *fantasías* by the author himself. (The last few measures of the sixth *fantasía* are reproduced on *Plate XXXVIII.*) Although Fuenllana does not explicitly state that these pieces were written for the five-string guitar, it can be satisfactorily demonstrated by playing the music that this, and not the *vihuela,* was the intended instrument.

The most comprehensive work on the five-string guitar was published in 1586 in Barcelona. This was a book by Juan Carlos Amat entitled *Guitarra española y vandola de cinco ordenes y de quatro,* previously mentioned in reference to the four-string guitar. However, it does have a section on the five-string type dealing with a new method of playing and contains several compositions for this instrument. (*Plate XXXIXa*)

Spanish works of art from this period support the existence of the five-string guitar in Spain. They include a wall painting in the Escorial Library dating from 1563 to 1584 (*Color Plate XLVIII*) and a stone carving over a doorway of the Convent of St. Stephen, in the Cloister of Kings, Salamanca, 1551. (*Plate XLVII*)

PLATE XLVIa
FRENCH GUITAR OF THE 16TH CENTURY KNOWN AS THE "RIZZIO GUITAR"

Cf. p. 77

PLATE XLVIb
DETAILS OF THE RIZZIO GUITAR

Cf. p. 77

PLATE XLVII
DETAIL OF SCULPTURE ON DOORWAY OF ST. STEPHEN'S CONVENT
1551

We have sufficient evidence to draw this conclusion: that the five-string guitar came to being as a result of the development and transformation of the four-string guitar. The tuning of the five-string instrument was A, D, G, B, E. That this tuning was the same one used by Fuenllana can be demonstrated by playing his music on the modern guitar, also tuned in the same manner. Apparently, therefore, the four-string type admitted the addition of a low string, not a high one as is sometimes claimed. Since the tuning of the four-string guitar was the same as that used on the first four strings of the modern guitar, the low A-string was obviously the later addition.

Some theorists are of the opinion that the fifth string was added for the first time by Vicente Espinel (1550-1624), a Spanish poet and musician. This theory must be discarded in view of the following evidence: the existence of highly developed five-string guitars (one of which is dated 1564) from the middle of the sixteenth century (at the above given date, Espinel would have been only fourteen years old), Fuenllana's publication of music for the five-string guitar in 1554, and, finally, Raimondi's engraving of Achillini and his five-string guitar appearing c. 1500. It is, therefore, clear that Espinel could not have been responsible for the addition of the fifth string to the four-string guitar and that the five-string guitar evolved much earlier in the fifteenth century.

Thus we have traced the emergence of the five-string guitar from its origin in Italy to its acceptance and increasing popularity throughout sixteenth century Europe.

Our knowledge of guitars that were extant at this time, together with the descriptions we have given of works of art from this period, show that the instrument achieved a high state of development, both in terms of its literature and in its artistic construction.

We have become aware of its use as solo instrument and in consort with instruments of other families. Its complete triumph, however, was still to come in the seventeenth century. This was to be substantiated by the amount of compositions written for the five-string guitar and by the number of guitars that were to survive from this century. These, in turn, would present a clearer and more unequivocal view of the guitar's continuing development.

PLATE XLVIII
DETAIL OF WALL PAINTING IN LIBRARY AT EL ESCORIAL, MADRID

Cf. p. 78

 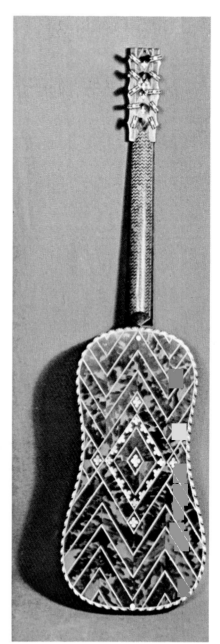

PLATE XLIX
GUITAR MADE BY RENÉ VOBOAM
1641

Cf. p. 84

CHAPTER 5

The Seventeenth Century

*T*he seventeenth century was the crest of a wave that had begun to rise in the Middle Ages. The patronage of the European nobility had brought to the guitar, first, recognition and then a measure of indispensability. From the courts of monarchs and the aristocracy, where it was played and listened to, it moved into the homes of wealthy families such as the Sforzas of Italy and permeated large segments of society. Inevitably, the number of composers for the instrument, along with guitarists and guitar makers, grew to staggering proportions. Improvements in methods of documentation have allowed their names and accomplishments to come down to us, and the historians' problem at this point becomes less a matter of searching for evidence than a matter of sifting through hundreds of manuscripts and other such historical sources for those contributions which are the most significant.

Among the distinguished royal personages who played the guitar was King Louis XIV of France, also known as "le roi soleil." He reigned, the epitome of the absolute monarch, from 1661 to 1715. His court stimulated and supported the activities of many great painters, sculptors and musicians of his day.

Musical life in this court centered to a great extent around the daily activities of the monarch himself. When he walked throught the halls of his sumptuous palace, Louis was followed by a band of musicians, diligently playing as they proceeded. Music accompanied his meals. It is said that when Louis heard a series of *Symphonies pour les soupers de roi,* written by Michel Richard de Lalande

(1657-1726), one of France's most outstanding composers, he liked it so much that he asked his court musicians to perform it again.

The popularity of the guitar in the court of Louis XIV was attested to by Anthony Hamilton in his *Memoirs of the Count de Gramont* (1665). According to Hamilton, the French ladies of the day kept their guitars as close at hand as their cosmetics. This observation is further supported by our own knowledge of several of these royal patronnesses of the guitar, one of whom was Princess Anne Louise Benedicte, who later married a son of Louis XIV.

It is known that Louis XIV himself played the guitar and regarded it as his favorite instrument. He had for his teacher one of the most important French guitarists known to us — Robert de Visée (c. 1650 c. 1725) who, beside instructing the king, also entertained in his court. In the introductory remarks to his first publication, *Livre de guitarre* (1682), de Visée draws attention to the popularity of the instrument in the French court and also gives the reader some interesting insights into his aims as a composer:

"So many people have applied themselves to the guitar and have given pieces for it to the public that I do not know if I could, in publishing mine, offer some novelty to the taste of the curious. However, I have worked only for that, and to be successful in that respect, I have attached myself to song [i. e., music] as much as possible to render them at least natural; knowing myself too well to pretend to distinguish myself by the strength of my composition, I have attempted to conform to the taste of knowing people, in giving to my pieces, as much as my weakness has been able to permit me, the turn of those of the inimitable Monsieur de Lully: I am persuaded that it is only in following him from very far, that my pieces have had the good fortune of being heard favorably by His Majesty and his court. This approbation which is so glorious to me, causes me to hope that my pieces will have some following."

The above quotation directs our attention to the great influence of Jean Baptiste Lully (1632-1687), one of the outstanding composers of all time, whose achievements contributed substantially to the form of the overture and to the style of operatic and vocal composition that was to dominate French music until the time of Rameau.

As a boy in Italy, Lully was given instruction in the

elements of music, and in guitar playing by an old monk who, besides being an ecclesiastic and a musician was, apparently, also a shoemaker. Coming to France in his early adolescence, Lully continued to play the guitar, and we even have reason to believe that he composed for the instrument. At the request of a courtier who was impressed with his guitar playing, Lully was given special instruction on the violin.

In all, the publications of de Visée were the above mentioned book of guitar (the five-course instrument) music dated 1682, two volumes of guitar works in 1686 and 1689, and a book of lute and theorbo music in 1716. The first of these publications also includes music in modern notation in two clefs which could be played on "the harpsichord, the violin and other instruments." These were put in, according to the author, at the request of his friends. The last suite for guitar required the tuning G♯-B-E-B-E. This interesting fact is enhanced by two others: the suite contains a French *chaconne*, and it is one of the earliest suites to include *menuet, gavotte* and *bourrée.**

Robert de Visée was also a lutenist, theorboist and singer. His son, François, succeeded him as a singer to Jean-Louis Marais in 1733.

Nicolas de Rosier was another important French guitarist who deserves to be mentioned. He was a chamber musician whose travels took him to England and the Netherlands. Most of his compositions were published in Amsterdam and in The Hague. Of these, the most outstanding are the eight "concerts" or *suites* and the twelve *overtures.* De Rosier claimed to have invented the so-called English guitar, which was not a guitar as we shall see, and was not, if De Rosier can be believed, English—at least not in origin.

Of a number of French noblemen who wrote for the guitar, one was Louis le Seigneur, who was in the employ of the famous Cardinal Richelieu. His work, entitled *Livre de Chansons en Tablature de Guitare,* was published by the House of Ballard in Paris. The book, dated 1626, is one of the earliest volumes of guitar music in the seventeenth century.

The names of several guitar makers during the Baroque period in France have been recorded. Some of these might be briefly discussed as representative.

---

*The present author has transcribed this Suite No. 6 into modern notation. It is one of the pieces in the "International Anthology for the Guitar."

The most significant was René Voboam, who was active in his craft toward the middle of the seventeenth century. He was obviously a craftsman of the utmost skill, representing the height of French instrument building in that century.

The only instrument by René Voboam known to us is a beautiful guitar dated 1641 and now in the Ashmolean Museum in Oxford. *(Color Plate XLIX)* It is an example of the more ornate style of instrument making. The five double strings are attached to an elaborate bridge decorated with alternating black and white diagonals. This motif, which is seen also on many guitars of the seventeenth and eighteenth centuries, surrounds the soundboard, neck and rosette of the Voboam guitar. The neck itself has a white scrollwork design on a black background. The back and sides of the soundbox have a fascinating variegated brown and tan pattern crisscrossed with white stripes. That this feature is present on the Rizzio guitar of the sixteenth century (identical shape and same pattern of black and white diagonals) indicates a steady continuity in French guitar workmanship.

In Paris, there was Alexandre de Voboam "le jeune", probably a relative of René Voboam. One of his fine guitars *(Color Plate L a)* is now in the Smithsonian Institution in Washington, D.C. This instrument was constructed in 1690. Originally it had five double strings but a later restoration gave it six single strings. The general appearance of this guitar is one of striking simplicity, as opposed to the more usual elaborate style.

Voboam had a son Jean who also built outstanding guitars with beautiful inlays.

Jean, also from Paris, was a guitar maker active in the second half of the seventeenth century. One of his guitars is in the museum of the Conservatoire National de Musique in Paris.

Guitars similar in construction to those of Voboam are shown not only in French art but in the art of other European countries as well. From works depicting the guitar, we have made a few selections.

The Concert by Valentin (1594-1632), a French artist who lived in Italy much of his life, shows a group of rowdy people seated around a table which has a Roman relief on one side. Besides a singer, there are three instrumentalists: a lutenist, a violinist and a guitarist. It is interesting to note that the guitar is part of this chamber ensemble. This painting is now in the Louvre Museum in Paris.

PLATE La
GUITAR MADE BY ALEXANDER VOBOAM
1690

Cf. p. 84

PLATE Lb
GUITAR MADE BY FRANCISCO LUPOT
1773

Cf. p. 132

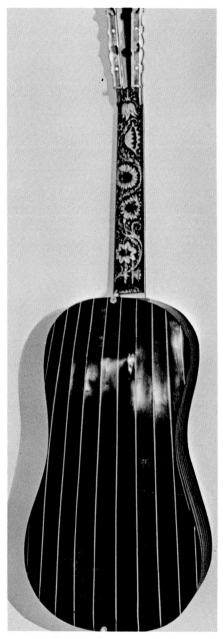

PLATE LI
GUITAR MADE BY JOACHIM TIELKE
1692

Cf. p. 90

Girl with a Guitar (1670), a famous Dutch painting by Jan Vermeer, shows the remarkable resemblance of the girl's instrument to that by Voboam. *(Color Plate la)* The features it has in common with the French guitar are the border pattern in white and black, the five double strings and the foliated bridge. A slight difference, however, is seen in the rosette, which in this case is flat and not three-dimensional.

An important aspect of technique may be gleaned from this painting. The Italian practice of resting the little finger of the right hand on the soundboard as shown here had apparently spread as far north as Holland. This picture shows first evidence in the use of the technique that was to be employed by nineteenth century guitarists such as Carcassi and Carulli, and which even Hector Berlioz later adopted for himself.

The Music Lesson (Plate LII) by Jacob Toorenvliet (1641-1710), another Dutch master, shows a jolly music teacher pointing to a music book held by his pupil, a robust young woman whose elbow rests on a table. With her left hand she supports a guitar of the *battente* type that is bare of decoration. This points to the fact that guitars were not exclusively of the highly ornate types exemplified by the Rizzio and René Voboam instruments. In plainer forms, they were also used by the people. However, it was the elaborate guitars of the nobility that made history at this point.

Undoubtedly there was a considerable number of works containing guitar music published in seventeenth century Holland. It will be recalled that the French composer Nicolas de Rosier had his music published in The Hague and Amsterdam. But we will cite the work of Isabel van Langhenhove as exceptional for having been written by a woman. Female guitarists were not unknown in Northern Europe as the paintings of Vermeer and Toorenvliet tend to imply, but Isabel is the only one from whose pen we have guitar music. She was probably Dutch, although the possibility of Flemish nationality cannot be entirely disregarded. Her single known work is a handwritten tablature book dated 1635.

Despite the apparent vogue for the guitar in Holland, it was in Germany that the instrument achieved its greatest popularity among the countries of Northern Europe. During the seventeenth century, Germany enjoyed a flowering of music under the aegis of the famous "Three S's," Heinrich Schütz (1585-1672), Samuel Scheidt (1587-1654) and

PLATE LII
The Music Lesson BY JACOB TOORENVLIET. 17TH CENTURY PAINTING

Johann Hermann Schein (1586-1630). Of these three, Schütz was the most important, particularly in the field of vocal and choral writing.

The scant documentation of seventeenth century German guitarists and composers has yielded a few names: Johann Gaspar von Döremberg, ambassador (from Hessen, Germany) to Paris, who was said to have completed in 1652 a book of guitar tablature; Athanasius Kircher (1602-1680), a Jesuit priest who taught at Würzburg University and included materials on the guitar in the *Musurgia Universalis* (Rome, 1650), a book on music theory. The guitar section of this work gives details on the tuning and stringing of guitars and lutes with accompanying illustrations.

The number of German guitars still in existence, however, compensates for the meagerness of information on German guitarists and guitar compositions.

The first known German-made guitar was built by Jacobus Stadler. It is dated 1624. *(Plate LIII)* It is in the *battente* form, with its typical curved, striped back. The beautifully executed designs on the front and back of the neck, as well as those surrounding the intricate three-dimensional rosette, show strong Italian influence. Indeed, at this time, the Italian school of guitar building had an almost overwhelming impact on Europe. The Stadler instrument retains its original string arrangement; that is, the five double strings do not terminate at the bridge but pass over it.

A seventeenth century guitar of an entirely different type is in the Metropolitan Museum of Art in New York. The maker of this instrument was a priest; the back of the guitar bears his name along with the instrument's province: *Pat. Iohannes fec. in apsam. (Plate LIV)* Father John of Apsam (Tirol) had decorated the back of the instrument with a crucifixion scene, a design unusual for a guitar. At the foot of the cross is a circle with a descending dove representing the Holy Spirit and, instead of the usual figures of St. John the Evangelist and the Virgin Mary, two angels, one praying and the other strumming a strange, rectangular harp. The entire picture is framed by rays emanating from Christ at the top. A seashell motif is at the bottom. The sides of the soundbox have peculiar curves ending in sharp points at the shoulders. The original tuning head seems to have been replaced by another in the eighteenth century style.

The most outstanding guitar maker not only of Germany

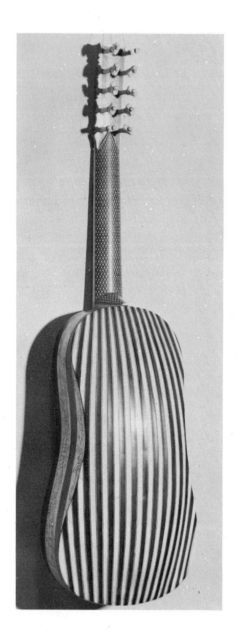

PLATE LIII
GUITAR MADE BY JACOBUS STADLER

1624

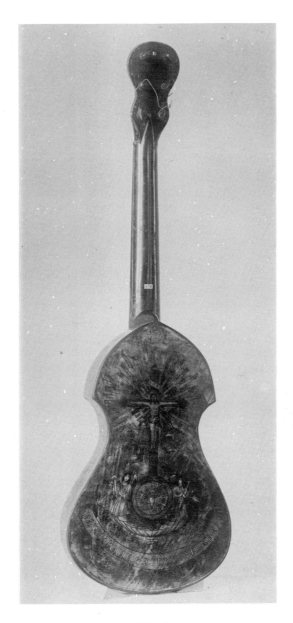

PLATE LIV
TYROLEAN GUITAR, MADE BY FATHER JOHN OF APSAM

17TH CENTURY

but of all Europe was Joachim Tielke of Hamburg, who lived from 1641 to 1719. His striking guitars were made and decorated with materials such as ivory, tortoise shell, ebony, gold and silver, mother-of-pearl, jacaranda wood, etc. The workmanship was consistently of the highest quality, unequalled even by the greatest Italian luthiers. It is quite probable, however, that on account of the elaborate and heavy designs covering his instruments, their tone was not as beautiful as their appearance.

Among Tielke's masterpieces is one with an unusually short neck and only eight frets. *(Plates LV & LVI)* The strings at one time numbered ten (five courses of two strings each) but a later restoration (the effects of which can easily be discerned by examining the back of the tuning head) changed the arrangement to six single strings. The back of the guitar has alternating black and white stripes interrupted by the curves at the sides. These are made of ivory with pictures of great beauty engraved on them. They represent scenes from Genesis. Three of them are shown on *Plate LVI*. At far left is an illustration of the story of Abel and Cain, the latter with his club lifted, about to strike his younger brother, who cowers on the ground. Next to it is a thin strip showing a man from the waist up. Below him is Tielke's inventory number, "1626." (These inventory numbers are so high because Tielke applied them not only to the completed instruments but to many accessories such as bows for violins. The inventory numbers should not be confused with dates.) To the right of this strip are other scenes, also from Genesis: Noah receiving instructions from God, who speaks from a cloud, and, immediately to the right of the mountain on which Noah kneels, the animals boarding the Ark in pairs. Among the members of this delightfully naive menagerie, elephants, dromedaries and cattle can be discerned. A thin border separates this picture from the next, which shows the Ark sailing away while the last naked sinners cling to the few mountain peaks still protruding above the flood waters.

Also outstanding is the Tielke guitar dated 1692, which is in the Gemeentemuseum at The Hague. *(Color Plate LI)* This instrument is in the *battente* form, and Tielke has used the usual stripe motif on the back of this instrument to decorate the sides as well. The back of the neck is covered with a design of strangely shaped flowers which, because they are found on most other Tielke instruments, may be considered a hallmark of his style. This *battente*

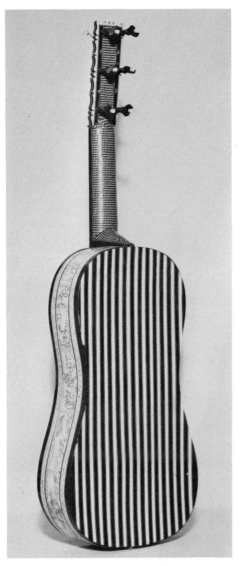

PLATE LV
GUITAR MADE BY JOACHIM TIELKE
17TH CENTURY

PLATE LVI
DETAIL OF TIELKE GUITAR SHOWN ON PLATE LV

guitar once had five double strings but these became six in number when the instrument was restored. The front is not authentic but the back, neck and sides of this guitar are superb examples of Tielke's craftsmanship.

The characteristic flowers are found in much greater profusion on another Tielke guitar in the Victoria and Albert Museum in London. *(Plates LVII & LVIII)* Even the sides and the design surrounding the rosettes are covered with them. The rosette itself is a remarkable example of the intricate three-dimensional carving used by seventeenth century luthiers on their work. The inlaid star around the rosette carries through the Tielke floral motif, which entwines six string instruments (guiternes, lutes, guitars, etc.). These probably were depictions of instruments previously made by the master. The back of this *guitarra battente (Plate LVIII)* is inlaid with tortoise shell, ivory and mother-of-pearl and is literally overflowing with flowers, vines and tiny mythological figures of cherubs and animals.

Tielke's consummate skill compels us to mention another instrument, also his handiwork. This beautifully ornamented *quinterna (Plate LIX)* was plucked with the fingers in the same manner as the guitar. Originally it had three double gut strings and two single ones covered with wire. Only four of the original eight pegs remain. The primary feature of this instrument is its fantastically intricate and beautiful workmanship. The back of the instrument is entirely covered with Tielke-type floral decorations surrounding mythological scenes. One side pictures Venus, goddess of love and beauty, admiring herself in a hand mirror while cupids, riding on two stylized dolphins, pull her chariot. A second scene shows Diana, goddess of the moon and of the hunt, bow and arrow in hand, reclining in her chariot drawn by two sprightly stags. The tuning box of the instrument is in the form of a human head, a design frequently used on the viola de gamba. Along the side of the neck is an inscription stating that the instrument was made in Hamburg by "IOAHIM: TIELKE." The number to the right, 1539, is the inventory number. The other numbers, "11'22'69", may be read as November 22, 1669, thus dating the instrument more precisely than any other Tielke known to us.

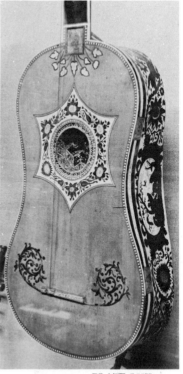

PLATE LVII
TIELKE GUITAR
IN THE
VICTORIA AND ALBERT
MUSEUM. FRONT

PLATE LVIII
TIELKE GUITAR IN THE VICTORIA AND ALBERT MUSEUM. BACK

PLATE LIX
QUINTERNA MADE BY JOACHIM TIELKE
1669

PLATE LX
GUITAR MADE BY ANDREAS OTT
1650

This tendency toward elaborate decoration, as manifested in the Tielke instruments, represents the height of German craftsmanship; it is comparable to that of the masters of the Italian Renaissance.

In summary, Joachim Tielke must be regarded as one of the most important instrument builders of all time, and his matchless work provides evidence that the guitar was highly regarded in seventeenth century Germany.

Apparently the guitar found its way into Eastern Europe as early as the mid-seventeenth century. In Czechoslovakia, an instrument (maker unknown) which appears to belong to this period shows that Czech luthiers attempted to adapt the *battente* type of guitar. In addition to the five double strings which the *guitarra battente* originally had, the Czech counterpart had another single string called "chanterelle" (from the French "chanter," to sing) and this string was used for playing the melodic line. To accommodate this string, a special tuning device was added to the tuning head, which was bent back perpendicular to the neck as on the lute.

Two guitars by Andreas Ott, instrument maker from Prague, substantiate the use of this instrument in Czechoslovakia and also show the impact of Italian influence. One, a *battente* type dated 1650 and now in London in the collection of William E. Hill & Sons *(Plate LX)*, has mother-of-pearl inlays around the rosette and a pattern of ovals in the same material on the fingerboard. This pattern has been used on many Italian guitars. The other Ott guitar in the National Museum in Prague carries the same arrangement of ovals on the fingerboard. Both instruments acquired six-strings after restoration.

Poland is represented in guitar history by Jakob Kremberg (b. 1650), poet, singer and composer from Warsaw who wrote music for the instrument. His book, *Musicalische Bemüths Ergötzung* (1689), consists of music for voice, bass and a quartet composed of lute, *angelique,* viola da gamba and guitar. According to the composer, these pieces could be performed either by voice with bass accompaniment, or by the instrumental quartet alone, or by voice and instruments together. Notation for all four instruments is in tablature. (See sample on *Plate LXI.*)

Among these four instruments, the least known is the *angelique,* also called *guitare angelique* or "angel's guitar." It has seventeen single metal strings and is actually more closely related to the lute and theorbo than to the guitar. It was quite popular during the seventeenth century.

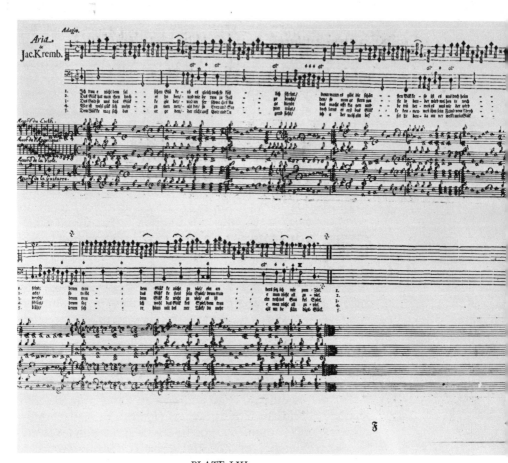

PLATE LXI
PAGE OF TABLATURE FROM *Musicalishe Bemüths Ergötzung* BY JAKOB KREMBERG
1689

The importance of Kremberg's work lies also in the information it gives us on the tuning of these instruments. The second string of the lute and *angelique* were to be the same pitch as the first strings of the guitar and viola da gamba, or equivalent to the pitch D on the clavichord. Thus the tuning of the guitar would be one tone lower than the tuning of our present day instrument.

Although the guitar was less popular in Spain than in Italy, and did not, in fact, attain the popularity that the *vihuela* had had in the previous century, some important works were published and a number of fine guitarists became known in that country.

The first Spanish work dealing with the guitar in the seventeenth century was the *Método para Aprender a Taner la Guitarra la Español* by Luis Brizeño, published in Paris in 1626. The author's writing and his reputation as a fine guitarist had a significant effect on the popularity of the instrument in France.

One of the prominent Spanish guitarists of the time, Francisco Corbera, dedicated his work *Guitarra Española y sus differencias de sonos* to Philip IV, king of Spain from 1621 to 1665. This powerful monarch also posed for Diego Velasquez, and his portrait became one of the most famous of this painter's works.

But the most notable Spanish guitarist of the seventeenth century was Gaspar Sanz. He was born in Calanda, Aragon and died in Madrid in 1710.

After earning a degree in theology from the University of Salamanca, Sanz went to Italy where he studied the guitar with Lelio Colista, to whom he referred in his later publications as "the Orpheus of his time." He also studied organ and music theory with Cristoforo Carisani. Subsequently Sanz became an organist at the King's Chapel in Naples. Upon his return to Spain, he published three books of guitar music which he engraved himself. The first book, entitled *Instrucción de música sobre la guitarra española,* has the following inscription on its first page: "Tomo I, sexta die Decembris anno 1674 . . . Gaspar Sanz, Invenit." The second book, *Libro segundo de cifras sobre la guitarra española,* gives its date as follows: "En Caragoza 1675." The third book, *Libro tercero de musica de cifras sobre la guitarra española,* was incorporated with the first and second books and the three together were published under the title of the first book and dated 1697.

The books contain the author's extensive instructions for improvisation and performance, using the two methods

of playing: strumming (or *taner de rasqueado*) and plucking (or *taner de punteado*). Sanz believed that the former
technique was most suitable for dance music. His particular
chord system was written in Italian notation and was
illustrated with two charts of consonant and dissonant
chords. The tuning he used was A-D-G-B-E.

In addition to being a guitarist and organist, Sanz was also
an accomplished composer. His music for guitar indicates
superior musicianship. Solo music occupies a large part of
his book. Also included are many dances and *passacaglias*
Much of the writing is in tablature, but there are several
short passages in modern notation. It will be recalled that
in standard tablature, the lines represent the strings of the
guitar and the numbers indicate the frets at which the
strings should be stopped. In the example on *Plate LXV,*
however, the lowest line stands for the highest string.
Timing is determined by the black notes above the staff.
The short black strokes visible on the bottom line at certain
intervals, particularly in the first three measures, conform
to the Italian method of notating strummed chords. This
specific example is indicative of Italian influence.

Many passages from the writings of Gaspar Sanz are
worth quoting. The following lines compare the guitar
with a woman and a rose:

"Others have discussed the perfection of this instrument, some saying that the guitar is a perfect instrument
and others saying that it is not; I say that it is neither
perfect nor imperfect, but as you make it, since the lack
of perfection or its presence depends on the player and
not on the guitar, since I have seen such marvels done
on one string where others would need a whole organ;
and for this reason, each one has to make the guitar
good or bad, since it is not like a lady who says 'look at
me but don't touch me.' It is like a rose, but very different from a real rose, since it does not die even if it is
touched frequently, because if a good player touches it,
it will produce new bouquets that, like sonorous odors,
will please the ear."

On the correct method for determining the quality of
the strings to be used, here is Sanz's suggestion:

"You will set the string in the guitar and after you
have tied it as much as you want, you will find the
twelfth fret, that is exactly the center of the instrument,
or the distance from the two bridges, and you will find
a mathematical proof in this way: play the string open,
and if you find that that makes an octave sound when

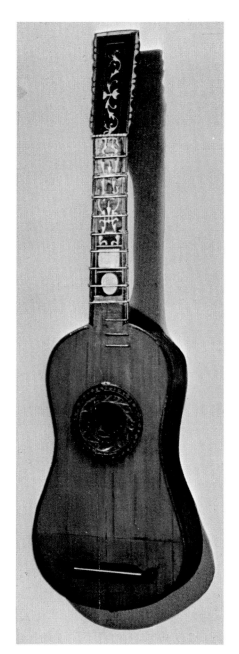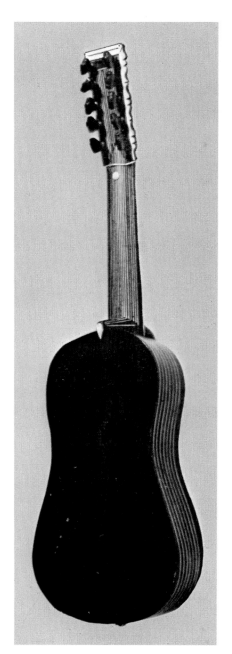

PLATE LXII
CHITARRINO MADE BY MATTEO SELLAS
C. 1620

Cf. p. 116

PLATE LXIII
GUITARRA BATTENTE MADE BY GEORGIO SELLAS
1627

Cf. p. 119

PLATE LXV
PAGE OF TABLATURE FROM *Libro tercero de musica* . . . BY GASPAR SANZ
1697

played with the finger on the twelfth fret, then the string is good, but if not, you better look for another one. You can fix this situation in a way, by putting the string upside down and this might fix the situation many times."

This method is still in use today.

The next significant publication after that of Sanz appeared in Madrid in 1677. Entitled *Luz y Norte Musical,* it was written by Lucas de Ribayaz, priest and canon in the church of Villafranca del Vierzo. It contains dances based on folk melodies.

Perhaps the most important Spanish composer of the seventeenth century was Don Francisco Guerau, a priest and musician in the court of Carlos II. His book *Poema harmonico compuesto de varias cifras por el temple de la Guitarra Española,* published in Madrid in 1694, contains twenty-five pieces: fifteen *passacaglias* and ten dances of various types including a *pavana* and a *galliard.* Among the more interesting of these compositions are the *passacaglias.* They are written in thirteen different keys, a greater number of tonalities than most modern composers of guitar music commonly use. They all end on an unresolved leading tone, thus allowing the performer to arrange the variations as he wishes. They all start in 4/4 measure but invariably change to 3/4 in the middle of the piece while retaining the initial 4/4.

The book was not written for beginners, as Guerau himself declared. However, he gave a series of instructions on tablature and ornamentation in addition to some very valuable comments on hand position and guitar technique which are interesting for historic and pedagogic reasons.

The following is a translation of one of the passages in Guerau's work:

"You require a good hand position, and for this you will notice, first, that the instrument should be held putting your right arm over it, so that the left hand does not hold it, because this hand should be free to move quickly up and down the fingerboard of the guitar.

"Secondly, that the left arm should be separated from the body in an arch, and the hand held in front of the frets making certain that the thumb does not show over the neck of the guitar as on the violin.

"Thirdly, that playing with the right hand when using the index and middle fingers should be done alternating them; because if the same finger plays too many consecutive, notes, the playing will not be fast and clean;

make certain that if you are playing from the first string, the playing should be continued with these fingers until you reach the fourth; and from the fourth on to the fifth with the thumb, playing with it all notes; and if you start with the lower strings proceeding to the higher notes, this should be done with the thumb up to the second string and from the second to the first with the index and the middle fingers.

"In addition, you must become accustomed to using the 'cejuela' [barré] by putting the index finger of the left hand over more or less all the strings, depending on your requirements, which is very necessary in order to play certain passages.

"Also see that you touch the strings with the tips of the fingers, and do not bend them in, but always keep your hand curved out."

This final remark by Guerau suggests that seventeenth century guitarists had a greater concern with the right hand position than they are usually given credit for, and that some two centuries before Tarrega, a considerably advanced technique had been developed. Several of Guerau's other points are also worth noting, particularly the reference to the thumb of the left hand which, according to him, should not project over the neck, and the description of the barré which even in the seventeenth century seems to have been an indispensable element in guitar technique.

The guitar continued to be depicted in the work of many artists. For instance in the *Temptation of Saint Jerome*, a wall painting in the Sacristy of Guadalupe (1638-1648), executed by Zurbarán, one of Spain's greatest seventeenth century painters, three plucked instruments are shown being played. One woman plays a guitar which closely approximates the modern instrument in size and shape. Another woman plays a harp, and behind her can be seen a "Portuguese guitar," an instrument related more to the cittern than to the guitar.

Geographic proximity and Spanish domination of Portugal (1580-1640) account to a large extent for the close connection between the music of the two countries. But it was the Portuguese monarch John IV (1603-1656) whose enlightened interest in music had the greatest effect in stimulating Portuguese composers. He founded the most comprehensive music library in seventeenth century Europe and wrote one of the earliest books of music criticism, *Defensa de la Musica Moderna,* in which he answers Bishop Cirilo Franco's objections against the *a capella* style of choral singing.

One of Portugal's most outstanding guitarists was Doisi de Velasco, who was employed by Philip IV of Spain. His first book, *Nuevo modo de cifra para taner la guitarra,* was published in Naples in 1640. A second work appeared five years later.

While in Madrid, Doisi met Espinel who, he claimed, invented the five-string guitar. Apparently the author was in error, since, as has been previously noted, this instrument had been in existence nearly half a century before Espinel's birth.

The fact that Doisi published in Naples, and that many other Iberian works were published in Italy, indicates that both Spain and Portugal had close cultural relations with seventeenth century Italy. It also indicates that the greater popularity of the guitar in that country led the Spanish and Portuguese masters to feel that they could realize higher profits if their books were printed in Italy rather than at home. Furthermore, many of the Spanish guitarists of this era, like Gaspar Sanz, worked in Italy.

That so many Iberian masters performed or had their compositions published there suggests that the guitar was of considerable significance in Italian musical life at this time. Indeed, the truly incredible number of composers and guitarists living during the Baroque period in Italy, and the fact that there are many more surviving instruments of this period here than in any other country, prove conclusively that this country was the center of the guitar world. We have already noted the widespread influence of Italian craftsmen in northern and eastern Europe.

In the first half of the seventeenth century, opera first became an important art form. The first great operas, works which still are among the masterpieces of Western music, were composed by Claudio Monteverdi (1567-1643). His first work in this form, *Orfeo,* was performed in Mantua in 1607. It met with immediate success and was followed by many others culminating in 1642 with *L'Incoronazione di Poppea.*

Similarly, important developments were taking place in instrumental music. In keyboard art, Girolamo Frescobaldi (1583-1643) excelled to such an extent that his first performance as organist at St. Peter's in Rome was reputedly attended by an audience of 30,000. Johann Sebastian Bach regarded him as one of his favorite composers and said that he learned a great deal from Frescobaldi's music.

Violin technique underwent revolutionary advancement

in the hands of Arcangelo Corelli (1653-1713) and Giuseppe Torelli (1658-1709). Corelli is regarded as the founder of modern violin technique and was among the earliest masters to employ double-stops and chords on the instrument. He perfected the form of the *concerto grosso*, an achievement to which Torelli also contributed.

It is, then, against a rich and varied musical background that we must consider the remarkable flowering of the guitar's popularity in Italy during the seventeenth century.

The most important factor which led to the popularity of the guitar in Italy and to the enrichment of its literature was the introduction from Spain of the *punteado* or plucked style of playing the instrument. It eventually replaced the strumming of chords that dominated the sixteenth century Italian practice. *Punteado* technique was in turn derived from the *vihuela* technique that the Spaniards adapted for their guitar.

Because the Spaniards were responsible for bringing this technique to Italy, it became known as *alla spagñuola* and the guitar thereafter came to be called *chitarra spagñuola,* although it was the same instrument that had been used for chord strumming. (A parallel situation has occurred today in the case of the so-called "folk guitar." — really no different in construction from the "classical" instrument but merely used for a different purpose.)

It must be noted that *punteado,* or plucked style of playing, was not unknown in Italy at the time of its arrival from Spain. Evidence for this is in a work by L'Academico Caliginoso (c. 1630), wherein were included several pieces without chords but with all the notes individually indicated by numbers. Caliginosc noted, apologetically, that these should be played "in the style of the lute." This style was considered inferior when applied to the guitar, but coming from Spain as an inherent part of guitar technique, it became acceptable to the Italians. Strictly speaking, therefore, Spain's contribution was not so much the introduction but rather the acceptability of the *punteado* technique in Italy.

Once the Italians had adopted the term *chitarra spagñuola,* they seem to have gradually widened its meaning so that for the rest of the seventeenth century it became a general term. The designation "Spanish guitar" persists to the present day as an extension of the seventeenth century usage. But it is interesting and slightly ironic that Italy should have "borrowed" the advanced style of guitar playing from Spain when the instrument itself had developed earlier in Italy.

The two essentially different techniques of guitar playing (strumming and plucking) co-existed in seventeenth century Italy. The *punteado* technique was expressed in tablature notation, with numbers to represent the frets required for the individual notes. The strumming of chords was indicated by a special notation developed by sixteenth and seventeenth century composers. This consisted of a chart of standard chords, each identified by capital letters. This chart, usually presented at the beginning of a book, was called *alfabeto*. The music could thus show only the letters and the guitarist, having studied the chart in advance, would know what chords were being referred to at any given point.

Plate LXVI illustrates the *alfabeto* as used by Domenico Pellegrini. In accordance with the practice of his time, he has used repeated letters with asterisks above them, as well as non-alphabetical symbols when the letters of the alphabet had been exhausted. He has also written arpeggiated chords below the *alfabeto*.

The tremendous number of surviving guitar compositions by seventeenth century Italian masters makes it difficult to choose a representative selection. We may, however, satisfy ourselves with a few items.

One of the first known works dealing with the guitar in Italy was published in 1606 in Florence. The book, *Nuova Inventione d'Intavolatura per sonare li balletti la chitarra Spagñuola senza numeri e note,* by Girolamo Montesardo, musical director of the Cathedral of Fano, contains music that is of little consequence, but the work is of interest as an illustration of guitar music early in the seventeenth century.

Another of the earliest Italian guitarists of the century was a nobleman from Palermo with the rather exotic name of Sigismondo d'India. He went to live in Florence in 1608 and in the following year the first of his many books, which included madrigals, villanelles and motets with guitar accompaniment, was published. In 1612, he became director of Chamber music under Count Carlo Emanuele of Savoy; in 1623 he went to Rome in the employ of Cardinal Moritz von Savoy. D'India was one of the first of many seventeenth century Italian guitarists who traveled widely and thus helped the spread of Italian influence.

Il primo libro d'intavolatura per la chitarra alla spagñuola by Benedetto Sanseverino is another early guitar work worth mentioning. It was published in Milan in 1622 and contains complex pieces in the form of *passacaglias,*

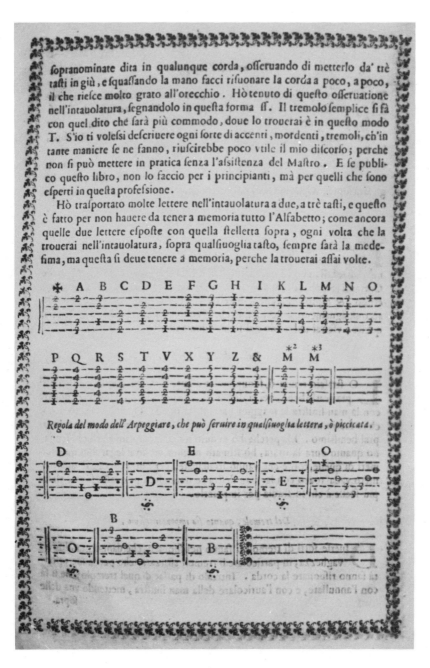

sopranominate dita in qualunque corda, osseruando di metterlo da' trè tasti in giù, e squassando la mano facci risuonare la corda a poco, a poco, il che riesce molto grato all'orecchio. Hò tenuto di questo osseruatione nell'intauolatura, segnandolo in questa forma ss. Il tremolo semplice si fà con quel dito che sarà più commodo, doue lo trouerai è in questo modo T. S'io ti volessi descriuere ogni sorte di accenti, mordenti, tremoli, ch'in tante maniere se ne fanno, riuscirebbe poco vtile il mio discorso; perche non si può mettere in pratica senza l'assistenza del Mastro. E se publico questo libro, non lo faccio per i principianti, mà per quelli che sono esperti in questa professione.

Hò trasportato molte lettere nell'intauolatura a due, a trè tasti, e questo è fatto per non hauere da tener a memoria tutto l'Alfabetto; come ancora quelle due lettere esposte con quella stelletta sopra, ogni volta che la trouerai nell'intauolatura, sopra qualsiuoglia tasto, sempre sarà la medesima, ma questa si deue tenere a memoria, perche la trouerai assai volte.

Regola del modo dell' Arpeggiare, che può seruire in qualsiuoglia lettera, ò piccicata.

PLATE LXVI
Alfabetto BY DOMENICO PELLEGRINI
1650

107

chaconnes, sarabandes, etc.

Early in the second quarter of the century, a guitarist named Foscarini published his work *Il primo, secondo e terzo libro della chitarra spagnuola.* (*Plate LXVII* reproduces its cover.) Although no date is given in the book itself, it has been tentatively attributed to the 1630's.

PLATE LXVII
COVER OF *Il primo, secondo e terzo libro della chitarra spagnola*
BY L'ACADEMICO CALIGINOSO (FOSCARINI)
C. 1630

Foscarini published under the *nom de plume* "L'Academico Caliginoso detto il Furioso" (the "smoggy" academician known as "The Furious"). Notwithstanding this pompous name, the music itself is of great lyrical beauty and reveals true harmonic inventiveness. Caliginoso gives instructions for tuning three different sizes of guitar and provides us with evidence for the popularity of the instrument in his time. According to him, the guitar is "today so much the fashion through all parts of the world, valued for some time by intelligent and experienced teachers." His book gives the usual instructions for playing the guitar, as well as several remarks on interpretation.

The most famous guitarist-composer of the century was Francisco Corbetta (Corbetti). Gaspar Sanz, in his work *Instrucción de musica sobre la guitarra española* (1674), refers to him as "the best of all," a statement that becomes more significant when one considers it was made in the seventeenth century, the Golden Age of guitar music, particularly in Italy.

Corbetta was born in Pavia, Italy in 1615. After traveling through Italy as a concert guitarist, he toured the rest of Europe with great success, his travels bringing him to many royal courts. He played for King Ferdinand III in Vienna in 1648, was employed by the Duke of Mantua (who later recommended him to Louis XIV of France), and played for Charles II who, upon becoming King of England, made Corbetta one of the grooms to the Privy Chamber of the Queen.

Corbetta was admired in London as a successful performer and a favorite teacher of the nobility. Samuel Pepys, in one of his diaries, describes a meeting with Corbetta in the home of the Duke of York. On this occasion, Pepys wrote, the guitarist played "most admirably . . . so well."

The most detailed description of Corbetta's virtuosity comes from the famous memoirs of the Count de Gramont (1621-1707).*

"There was a certain foreigner at court famous for the guitar; he had a genius for music and he was the only man who could make anything of the guitar; his style of playing was so full of grace and tenderness that he could have given harmony to the most discordant instruments. The truth is, nothing was too difficult for this foreigner. The King's relish for his compositions had brought the instrument so much into vogue that every person played on it well or ill . . . This Francesco (Corbetta) had composed a saraband which either

*Edited by Sir Walter Scott.

charmed or infatuated every person; for the whole guitarery at court were trying at it, and God knows what a universal strumming there was."

Corbetta remained a favorite of Charles II until the King's death, in 1685. In the revolution of 1688, Corbetta fled to Paris where he died in 1689.

His most important musical contributions were his compositions. His first publication was *De gli scherzi armonici* (Bologna, 1639). His second, published in Milan in 1643 when he was twenty-eight years old, was a book entitled *Varii capricii per la chitarra spagñuola* and dedicated to Corbetta's patron, "His Serene Highness, Carlo, Duke of Mantua and Monferrato." *(Plate LXVIII)* In 1670 his book *La Guitarra Royalle* was published in Paris and in 1674 another collection of his compositions came out under the same title.

Corbetta used three different types of tablature to notate his music. In the first book, *alfabeto* predominates. In the second book, he used mixed tablature, that is, *alfabeto* and single notes indicated by numbers. *(Plate LXIX)* For his Parisian publications of 1670 and 1674, he used French tablature in which the notes are represented by small letters.

The forms of his compositions varied — *toccatas, passacailles, sinfonias,* etc.; but the most significant are his suites, which consisted only of the *Almanda, Courrente* and *Sarabanda.* These were the earliest suites of the Baroque period, and although Corbetta himself did not use the term "suite," he grouped the pieces in the above order and indicated they were to be played as a set.

PLATE LXVIII
PORTRAIT OF FRANCESCO CORBETTA
FROM HIS BOOK *Varii capricii per la chitarra spagnuola*
1643

Among the distinguished colleagues of Corbetta, Giovanni Battista Granata also achieved international renown. He was the most prolific of the seventeenth century masters. His compositions were published in seven volumes, each of a substantial size. Book four alone has one hundred and sixty-three pages. The first volume was published in 1646, the last in 1684. The compositions are noteworthy for their musical value and complexity. In Granata's lifetime they had a reputation for being difficult, as the composer himself admitted. The pieces for solo guitar include *preludes, toccatas, correntes* and many others. The chamber works call for combinations such as violin, guitar and continuo (Book IV), and violin, viola and guitar (Book V). A page of tablature from the former *(Plate LXX)* has the violin part and continuo bass in modern notation. The guitar part, placed between the violin and continuo parts, is in tablature.

A reproduction from Book IV shows Granata playing an extremely interesting guitar. *((Plate LXXI))* The tuning pegs are clearly nine in number, the same as on the instrument in Corbetta's book of 1643.*(Plate LXVIII)* Few surviving guitars from this period have this arrangement, but we can be certain how the strings were distributed. It may be recalled that in the sixteenth century Italy had a seven-string guitar with three courses of two strings each plus one single string. The same arrangement was extended to the seventeenth century and it is beyond a doubt that the nine-string guitar had four courses of two strings each plus one single string — the first one.

Judging from the numbers in the tablature (Book IV, page 19), the guitar for which Granata wrote evidently had sixteen frets, which was considerably more than the guitars of that time usually had. Indeed, Granata tells us that he added frets to his guitar to make possible the playing of higher notes.

Granata also provides evidence for the existence of a "theorbo-guitar," or guitar with extra bass strings. In one of his books (Book IV), there is a series of six pieces for a five-course guitar with seven extra bass strings whose tuning, in terms of modern pitch, is as follows: sixth string in G; seventh in F; eighth in E; ninth in D; tenth in C; eleventh in B; twelfth in A.

Shortly after Granata's first book there appeared in Italy a collection of charming compositions by Domenico Pellegrini entitled *Armoniosi concerti sopra la chitarra*

PL.
PAGE OF TABLATURE FROM *Varii Capricii p*
1

spagñuola (1650).* In its introduction, Pellegrini offers instructions "to those who study the Spanish guitar."

"If by your courtesy or curiosity you would like to play these compositions of mine, I have some necessary advice since my book cannot be used without the help of the teacher. And as it was not made to perform miracles, it is necessary to read the notes [rules] that I have written for those who already know tablature; and having been taught for some time they will profit by reading them."

This collection of thirty-eight pieces includes compositions in the form of *brando, alemanda, corrente, toccata* and others. Among them is a *passacaglia* which is nineteen pages long. The *alfabeto* of this book (see *Plate LXVI*) has been discussed previously.

We should also mention Ludovico Roncalli, who was

---

*Editor's note: The present author's collection of Pellegrini's music published by Franco Colombo, Inc. (New York) will, it is hoped, go far toward establishing Pellegrini as a true master. Other collections by Mr. Bellow in the Colombo catalog include works by A. Le Roy, G. Brayssing, Carlo Calvi, F. Corbetta, G. B. Granata, L'Academico Caliginoso, Gaspar Sanz and F. Guerau.

...ara Spagnuola BY FRANCESCO CORBETTA

probably connected with the court of Bologna. His first opus was published in 1692 in Bergamo and was dedicated to Cardinal Panfilio, then the papal legate in Bologna. Nine suites comprise the book entitled *Capricci Armonici sopra la Chitarra Spagñuola.* They are written in mixed tablature, that is the *alfabeto* (for strummed chords) and the *punteado* (single notes designated by numbers) were combined within a single composition. Roncalli was probably influenced by the music of Granata and Corbetta, who both taught at Bologna for some time.

The Italian guitarists thus far discussed were all of superior calibre, but many other guitarist-composers, though less distinguished, deserve mention for having written much charming music and for thus having enriched the literature of the guitar.

Carlo Calvi wrote *Intavolatura di chitarra e chitariglia,* a book published in 1646. It is divided into two sections: the first consists solely of *alfabeto,* the second of pieces notated by numbers for *punteado* technique. Apparently Calvi was the only one among his contemporaries who wrote pieces that were exclusively for *punteado* technique. The other composers of his time used mixed tablature. Like Caliginoso, Calvi included in his book detailed instructions for tuning guitars of three sizes.

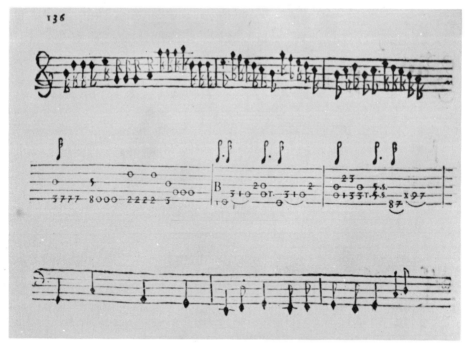

Giovanni Bottazzari Mantovano wrote *Sonate nuove per la chittarra spagnola,* which appeared in 1663. The significant feature of this work is that, besides the usual guitar tuning, it gives no less than six other tunings invented by Mantovano himself, some of them harmonically interesting. There are as many as sixty pieces in this book.

Many important guitarists, as previously noted, traveled throughout Europe carrying with them the guitar and its music. One such musician was Orazio Clementi (1637-1708), a theorbist in the court orchestra of Vienna and a composer of guitar music. Seven of his guitar pieces, some in the form ot *chaconnes* and *passacaglias* "alla spagnuola" are known to be in the National Library of Vienna.

Nicola Matteis, an Italian guitarist who lived toward the end of the seventeenth century, taught, performed and composed in London. He apparently gained enough proficiency in English to translate for publication a work he had written earlier, *Le false consonanze della musica. Per toccar la chitarra sopra alla parte in breve.* The English version was entitled *The false consonances of musick . . .*

The wanderlust of these musicians must have exceeded that of the troubadours of the earlier days. One of them, Antonio del Mazzara, went as far as Jerusalem to be able to live, so he claimed, a life of "more philosophorum." He wrote a book entitled *Chitarra septem chordorum.* The seven strings referred to in the title would be the three double strings and one single string of the four-course guitar.

Composers who were not primarily guitarists also wrote for the instrument. Of these perhaps the most illustrious was Steffano Landi (1590-1655), the first composer of the Roman opera school. Among his works are a series of sixty-one songs of which six have guitar accompaniment notated in tablature.

Orazio Tarditi, an organist at St. Michael's Church in Murano, was also a composer of the Roman school. He used the guitar in church singing, at that time a novel function for the instrument. In a way it may be viewed as a reversion to the practice in Babylonian temples three thousand five hundred years before.

In northern Europe, women apparently also had part in the guitar history of this period. A lady guitarist from Italy, Franzisca Ambrosius, was known as a skillful musician who won acclaim for her performance on the guitar.

Aside from composers and their music for the guitar,

there were scholarly works written about the instrument and its performers. A book on sixteenth century Italian guitarists, singers and lutenists entitled *Della practica musica vocale e strumentale* was written by Scipione Cerreto and published in Naples in 1601.

The plethora of Italian seventeenth century manuscripts and published works is matched by a large number of surviving guitars found in museums throughout the world. Unlike the guitars from the north with their rather uniform designs and patterns, the Italian guitars displayed a great variety of ornamentation. The distinctive artistry of various makers gave rise to a number of schools of guitar making, some of which rose to great prominence in the course of the seventeenth century.

One of these schools is represented by two guitars now in London. They were built by unknown makers in the beginning of the century. *(Plates LXXII & LXXIII)* Both have flat backs, bridges terminating in curving foliage, and shapes that are very much alike. Both also used to have five double strings. Restoration, however, has caused some changes. One of the guitars now has six single strings and both instruments have lost their carved rosettes.

The difference between the two instruments lies mainly in the designs decorating them. The guitar which now has six strings *(Plate LXXIII)* has a checkerboard motif all over the back and sides of the soundbox, on the back of the neck and behind the tuning head. These little squares are repeated around the rosette and on the border of the soundboard and fingerboard. Here, however, they are made from mother-of-pearl. The same material has been used for the trefoil design under the bridge and for a series of ovals on the fingerboard. These ovals are similar to those on the guitar by Andreas Ott of Prague *(Plate LX)* built fifty years later.

The other guitar *(Plate LXXII)* has a series of five bands running lengthwise down the back of the soundbox, elegant vine tendrils weaving around them. Similar bands are seen on the sides. Both front and back of the neck are bare, except for a thin border resembling the bands on the back. This border continues around the soundboard. The same kind of interweaving stripes surround the rosette.

Other guitars are of interest both in themselves and because of the information they give us on the guitar makers and their craft.

A *chitarrino* (or small guitar) from the first half of the seventeenth century (c. 1620) is shown on *Color Plate*

PLATE LXXII
GUITAR WITH FIVE DOUBLE STRINGS. ITALIAN SCHOOL
C. 1600

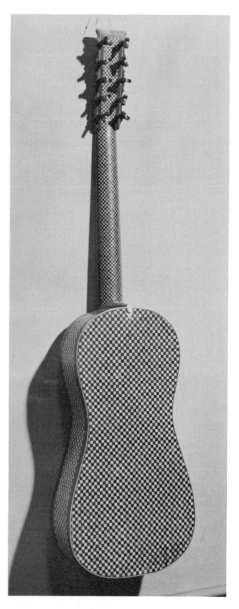

PLATE LXXIII
GUITAR WITH FIVE DOUBLE STRINGS. ITALIAN SCHOOL
C. 1600

LXII. This instrument is only thirty-five inches in length. Although it is unsigned, it is undoubtedly the work of a well-known Italian master of the time, Matteo Sellas, whose workshop was located in Venice. That it is the work of this luthier is proved by the presence of two marks at the bottom of the fingerboard. One, unmistakably the coat of arms used by Sellas' patron; the other, a crown which Sellas is known to have used as a trade mark. Above the insignia, the fingerboard is decorated with an ivory design reminiscent of that on so many sixteenth and seventeenth century instruments, among them the guitar on *Plate XLVI*. Although the soundboard of the *chitarrino* is entirely bare, the rosette is beautifully carved in three dimensions. The metal frets and the back, made of jacaranda wood, were added at a later date when the instrument was restored.*

An amazingly ornate *guitarra battente* was made in 1627 *(Color Plate LXIII)* by Georgio Sellas, brother and colleague of Matteo Sellas. Its rosette is carved with the same careful attention to detail that has been noted so frequently. Little wisps of foliage are strewn here and there on the soundboard, while more elaborate ivory leafage covers the sides and back. Ivory was also used for the rectangular plaques on the fingerboard as well as for the tuning head. The instrument retains its original arrangement of five double strings passing through the bridge, but it would not be worthwhile to play this guitar, as the heavy ornamentation would, in all probability, dampen the sound.

The same school of guitar construction is represented by an Italian instrument now in Paris. *(Plate LXXIV)* This *guitarra battente* bears some similarity to the previous one made by Georgio Sellas and it was possibly the work of a very skilled contemporary of the master. It is profusely decorated with foliage that twists and turns over the back, the sides, the fingerboard and tuning head. The same design surrounds the rosette and is duplicated across the bridge. The carving of the rosette consists of two six-point stars, one smaller than the other, and so placed as to give the illusion that they are receding into the depths of the soundbox. The original arrangement of the strings has been retained, although in this case they pass over rather than through the bridge. It dates from c. 1620.

Since I have continually referred to the beautiful three-dimensional rosettes of the seventeenth century guitars, it would probably be desirable to present one in greater detail. This is illustrated on *Plate LXXV*. It belongs to a *guitarra*

*This instrument was carefully examined by the author.

PLATE LXXIV
CHITARRA BATTENTE. ITALIAN SCHOOL
C. 1620

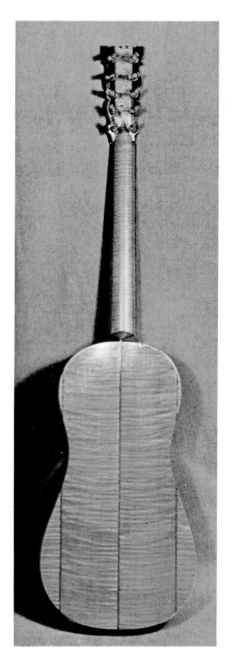

PLATE LXIV
GUITAR MADE BY ANTONIO STRADIVARIUS
1680

Cf. p. 121

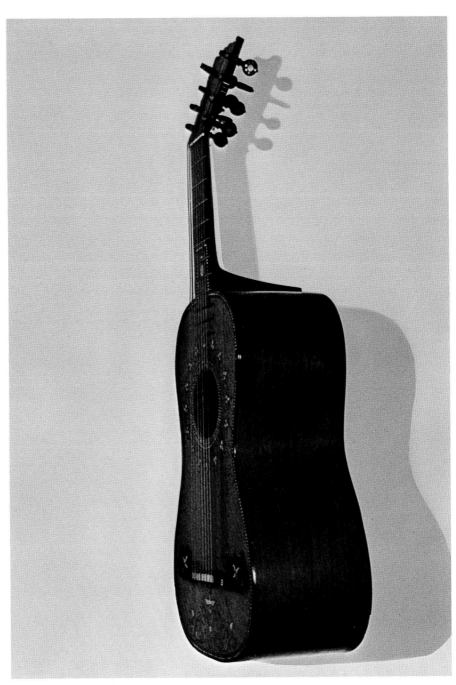

PLATE LXXIX
GUITAR MADE BY FRANCISCO SANGUINO
1759

Cf. p. 135

battente of that period, which is now in the Victoria and Albert Museum in London. A description would be superfluous as this beautiful work of art speaks for itself.

An instrument apparently unique in its ornamentation was built in Venice in 1650 *(Plate LXXVI)* and can now be found in London at the Horniman Museum. It is made almost entirely of ebony. Covering the soundboard is a delicate lace-like filigree pattern. The fingerboard is decorated with alternating black and white triangles, the white ones made of mother-of-pearl. The tuning pegs are of carved ivory and they frame several larger triangles of the same type as those on the fingerboard and around the soundboard.

Antonio Stradivarius (1644-1737) of Cremona, the most famous Italian instrument maker of the seventeenth century, is best known for his matchless violins, violas and cellos, but he was also known to have built harps, *ceteras* and guitars. Two of his guitars are known to us. One *(Color Plate LXIV)* was acquired in London in 1880 by William Hill and Sons, whence it passed to its present owner, The Ashmolean Museum in Oxford, England. In marked contrast to the ornate guitars previously described, this instrument exhibits a classic restraint and elegance equaled only by modern luthiers. The absolutely plain soundboard is enriched by a flat rosette carved with interweaving double lines. The coat of arms of Stradivarius' noble client is inscribed toward the bottom of the fingerboard. On the back of the tuning head is the inscription: ANT. S. STRADIVARIUS CREMONENs F, 1680.

The other known Stradivarius guitar was dated the following year, 1681, and is made of different woods: pine for the top and rosewood for the back and sides of the soundbox. This instrument bears the following inscription: *Questa e del Signor Canobio da Vendere,* which refers to Frederico Canobio, an amateur guitarist of the seventeenth century.

Judging from the quality of these two guitars by Stradivarius, the great craftsman must have had considerable experience in this area and may have built other guitars. It is certainly hoped that some of these will come to light in the future.

Having thus followed the development of the guitar, its use and its music in seventeenth century Europe, we are struck by the instrument's enormous popularity at this time, especially in Italy where the greatest amount of music and the greatest number of guitars were produced. The impor-

PLATE LXXV
DETAIL OF THREE-DIMENSIONAL SOUND HOLE ON ITALIAN GUITAR
17TH CENTURY

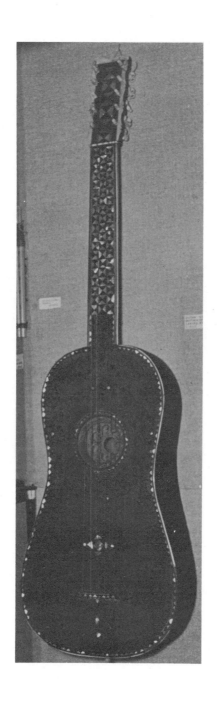

PLATE LXXVI
GUITAR MADE FROM EBONY. ITALIAN SCHOOL
C. 1650

tance of this century to the history of the guitar will undoubtedly be further realized as more of this music is studied and transcribed into modern notation.

CHAPTER 6

The Eighteenth Century

*I*n the seventeenth century, Italy was the undisputed center of the guitar world and retained this position of leadership until the succeeding century. By this time, however, a challenge began to come from the north. Germany, where the guitar had had a measure of popularity in the 1600s, became increasingly active in this particular musical field, and before long it had accumulated an impressive number of guitarists and composers for the instrument whose achievements rivaled those of the Italians.

German baroque music had reached a culminating point in this century. Masters such as Johann Pachelbel (1653-1706) and Vincentius Lübeck (1654-1740) excelled in those compositions for organ which were to pave the way for the music of Johann Sebastian Bach (1685-1750). This century was also to witness a great revival of interest in the lute, encouraged by composers like Ernest Gottlieb Baron (1696-1760), who wrote for the instrument. Bach himself, in addition to his numerous cantatas, Passions, orchestral suites, concerti and other instrumental and vocal pieces, composed for the lute, inspired by his friend Sylvius Leopold Weiss (1686-1750), whose mastery of the instrument was matched only by the beauty of his music.

This revival enriched the literature for the lute and caused developments in the instrument that eventually led to the rise in the popularity of the guitar. The lute, increasingly, became a complex instrument, arriving at a point where it had no less than twenty-four strings: eleven double and two single. As it accordingly required more skill and training for performance, and as the problems involved in the technique of playing it increased, it became less and less accessible. It is no exaggeration to say that it took more time to tune the instrument than to perform a piece on it. People who realized this turned to the guitar.

In this context it is interesting to note that several of the important lutenists of the day were also guitarists. Rudolph Straube is a case in point. He was a student at the Leipzig University and was taught by J. S. Bach himself. He played lute concerts in London where he died in 1780. Among his compositions are three sonatas for guitar and two for lute.

The growing number of guitarists was matched by an increasing number of composers for the instrument. Before discussing those composers who paid special attention to the guitar, we might mention that George Frederick Handel wrote a cantata in which the guitar is used. This early work, *No se emendera jamas (cantata spagñuola),* is scored for soprano, guitar and continuo.

A number of composers wrote for solo guitar: Johann Arnold (1773-1806), who was also a cellist; Friedrich Baumbach (1753-1813), who wrote *variations, preludes, etudes, romanzas* and *rondos;* and Johann Christian Franz (1762-1814), whose compositions included *etudes, fantasias, marches,* etc., were some of these. But the most important aspect of German guitar music of the eighteenth century is the use of the instrument in a variety of chamber ensemble combinations.

Baumbach, mentioned above, also wrote music for guitar and piano. Karl Andreas Göpfert (1768-1818) was a clarinet player who seems to have outdone his colleagues in the originality of his instrumental groupings: guitar and flute; two guitars and flute; guitar and bassoon; guitar, viola and bass. Franz Xaver Süssmayer (1766-1803), a friend of Mozart and once a conductor of the National Theater, Vienna, composed a quintet for violin, guitar, oboe, horn and cello.

Other names (some of them belonging partly to the eighteenth and partly to the nineteenth century) deserve to be included in the list of significant composers of chamber music with guitar. Among these are Placidus von Camerloher (1720-1776), an organist, lutenist and violinist; Gottlieb Heinrich Köhler (1765-1833), flutist and teacher, who also composed for guitar solo; Joseph Martin Kraus (1756-1792), who wrote for guitar and piano; Bernhard Romberg (1767-1841), a violinist and guitarist who concertized in England and Spain.

An important theoretical publication about the guitar, *Neu eröffneter theoretischer und praktischer Music-Saal,* by Joseph Friedrich Bernhardt Kaspar Majer, may be singled out because it contains the earliest known reference to a six-string guitar. Since the musical examples given are in Italian tablature, it may be supposed that at this time the six-string guitar was a uniquely Italian instrument. Its tuning, according to Majer, was D-A-D-F♯-A-D.

When and how the six-string guitar was adopted in Germany cannot be precisely ascertained. Majer's book, which was written in 1732, indicates an awareness of the instrument in that country. We do know that the Duchess Amalia von Weimar brought a five-string guitar from Italy to Weimar in 1788. This instrument served as model for some of the early efforts of the celebrated guitar maker Jacob August Otto (1760-1829). The resulting instruments became so popular within the next ten years that Otto was flooded with more orders than he could meet. He is therefore believed responsible for the popularity of the guitar in southern Germany.

In the last decade of the eighteenth century, Otto was ordered by a certain conductor from Dresden (by the name of Naumann) to add to his five-string guitar a sixth string — the bass — in accordance with Italian practice.

Other guitar makers in Germany include George Philippe Althenn of Frankfurt-Am-Main. One of his guitars, dated 1750, has survived to the present day. Martin Grieser worked in Dresden at the end of the century. Michael Stadlmann and Matthew Hummel worked in Nürnberg from 1694 to 1715. One of Hummel's highly prized guitars was at one time in the former Imperial Museum of Russia.

The guitar, having gained popularity in Germany, moved to the countries farther north. In Denmark, Peter Schall (1762-1820), cellist and brother of the famous ballet composer Klaus Schall, achieved mastery of the guitar and composed songs and choruses with guitar accompaniment.

Belgium produced a number of fine guitarists, among whom was François le Cocq, a violinist with the Brussels Court Orchestra. He wrote numerous guitar works in French tablature and had them published, under the name *Recueil des pièces de guitarre,* in Brussels. At a later date, Le Cocq published an anthology of guitar music by seventeenth century masters: Derosier, Corbetta, Sanchez, Luc, de Lelio, de Visée, Zavala, Granata and others.

A Belgian guitar maker of the eighteenth century, D.

Lucx, was briefly discussed by Domingo Prat in his well-known work, *Diccionario de Guitarristas.*

In Holland, the Cuypers family of renowned instrument makers was also making guitars. Theirs became a flourishing house, with representatives at The Hague and Amsterdam. A "nine-string guitar" by Jan C. Cuypers (1719-1806?), one of the members of this family, may be mentioned as an interesting novelty.

Another guitar maker in Holland was F. J. Delannoy. One of his guitars has five double strings and bears the inscription: "F. J. Delannoy le fils à Bruxelles, 1777." This represents a relatively late date for this type of guitar. The instrument is now in the Brussels Museum.

The interest shown in the guitar in the northern countries was equaled to that in the countries of the eastern part, such as Bohemia, Czechoslovakia and Russia.

Johann Baptist Wanhal (1739-1813), a Bohemian who lived in Venice and Vienna for periods of his life, composed for chamber ensemble which included the guitar. Among the various instrumental combinations for which he wrote were guitar, violin, viola and cello; violin and guitar; piano and guitar. He was a friend of Carl Ditters von Dittersdorf.

Another Bohemian, Alexander Miksch (?-1813), was a French horn player with the Dresden Court Orchestra, a virtuoso guitarist and a composer. Among his compositions is the *Thema mit sechs Variationen für Guitarre.*

In Czechoslovakia, the tradition of guitar playing continued to be reaffirmed by composers like Heinrich Dringeles (whose *Variazionen über ein Tiroler Lied,* opus 1, for solo guitar was published in Prague) and by guitar makers like Jean Bourgard (Burghardt), who worked in the same city in the second half of the century producing, in addition to guitars, a large variety of mandolins, basses, lutes, English guitars and a "mechanical guitar."

It was in the late eighteenth century that the guitar began to establish itself firmly in the musical environment of Russia. Although it had been known there in various forms for many years, the guitar attained prominence only in the nineteenth century; hence, the musicians who were primarily responsible for making the history of the guitar in Russia will be discussed in a subsequent chapter. But the pioneers in guitar building began their work in the eighteenth century. One of these was Ivan Andreyevitch Batov, who worked for Count Sheremetyeff, an ardent patron of music and arts. Batov's workshop was established in Ulm

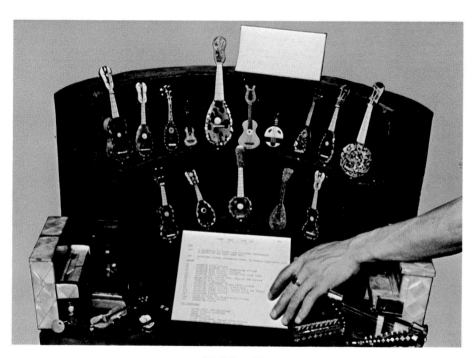

PLATE XCIV
THE "QUEEN'S BAND" OF MINIATURE INSTRUMENTS

Cf. p. 149

PLATE XCV
GUITAR WITH "C" HOLES
MADE BY LES FRERES MAUCHANT

Cf. p. 174

in 1780. From it flowed a variety of musical instruments including guitars, balalaikas, violins and cellos.

While it is true that many of the guitarists thus far mentioned were members of court orchestras, it was in France that the guitar attained the status of instrument *par excellence* for the nobility. Here, the tendency to associate the guitar with elegance in sound became especially marked and was subsequently reflected in the many charming works of art which picture the instrument. The most celebrated are the paintings of Antoine Watteau (1684-1721), whose delightful canvasses present a panorama of elegant courtly life. Young men and women stroll about in sweeping pastoral settings. They are frequently shown playing the guitar, the instrument so carefully drawn by the painter that we can usually distinguish the pegs for five double-strings, the foliage spray on either side of the bridge, and the ubiquitous black and white border. The guitarists of Watteau, however, seem to be more interested in the elegance of their appearance than in aspects of their performance.

Other French artists who pictured the guitar in their *oeuvre* were Jean Baptiste Pater and Ollivier. The former has left a sketch in which a Watteau-like figure languidly plucks his instrument. The latter, in a work entitled *Le Thé à l'anglaise chez la Princesse de Conti* (1766), shows the guitar with a cello and a harpsichord.

The French, besides representing guitars in their art, also produced art work on their guitars. The instrument shown on *Plate LXXVII* was màde in the eighteenth century in Paris by a craftsman named Bernard. It has a picture on its back done entirely in gold and brown tones. At the very top of this classical scene, above the tallest clump of trees, can be discerned the title of the painting: "L'AMOUR INGENIEUX."

The changes in decoration and ornament as exemplified by Bernard's guitar did not, however, constitute a departure in the construction of the instrument. The French school of guitar making continued to develop gradually, following the same methods of construction used earlier and represented by the sixteenth century Rizzio Guitar (*Color Plates XLVI a & b*), and by the seventeenth century René Voboam instrument. (*Plate XLIX*) The continuity is demonstrated by a number of eighteenth century instruments. One of these, from the turn of the century, is a guitar by Jean Baptiste Champion, now in the Boston Museum of Fine Arts. (*Plate LXXVIII*)

PLATE LXXVII
GUITAR MADE BY BERNARD OF PARIS
18TH CENTURY

PLATE LXXVIII
GUITAR MADE BY BAPTISTE CHAMPION
C. 1800

While Champion is known to have built six-string guitars, he also used the traditional arrangement of five double strings as on this particular instrument. The factor that most obviously links this guitar to its classical French predecessors is the border decoration of alternating ebony and ivory diagonals, here repeated around the rosette. The rosette itself, however, instead of being elaborately carved out of wood in three dimensions is covered with a parchment rose. Several of the original gut frets are still attached to the neck.

An example of the eighteenth century six-string guitar is an instrument made by Francisco Lupot. *(Color Plate Lb)* It is dated 1773. The tuning head in the shape of an inverted guitar soundbox was already quite popular in the eighteenth century, and is of the type that was to become almost universal in the nineteenth. Lack of decoration around the sound hole is a notable feature inasmuch as it reveals the increasing concern with functional rather than decorative design.

A more unusual variety of guitar seems to have been developed at this time — the bass guitar. This instrument had a series of extra strings off the neck attached to a separate tuning box. The type is exemplified in one built by Gerard J. Deleplanque, 1782 *(Plate LXXX),* who worked in Lille in the second half of the eighteenth century. This bass guitar has six single strings on the neck and four bass strings on the side, the total number of strings being ten. This type of ten-string guitar was later to become extremely popular in the second half of the nineteenth century when it became known as the *chitarra decachorda.* It survived to the early part of the twentieth century.

The guitar makers discussed above are only a few of the most important in a century that saw the culmination of the guitar's popularity in France. Toward the end of the century, the revolution of 1789 forced into exile many nobles and caused the death of countless others. The fall of the nobility, the class which had provided the guitar with its greatest patronage, fortunately did not lead to obscurity for the instrument. On the contrary, in time it climbed to a higher level of popularity as a result of its adoption by the masses. The revolution, therefore, did not prove detrimental to the guitar. In effect, it merely transferred the patronage of the instrument from the nobility to the common man.

Of course the instrument could hardly have attained the degree of favor it enjoyed before and after the revolution

PLATE LXXX
BASS GUITAR MADE BY GERARD J. DELEPLANQUE
1782

without the efforts and accomplishments of the musicians—performers and composers.

One of these was Trille Labarre, a virtuoso on the guitar who lived in Paris toward the end of the century. He wrote music for guitar solo, for guitar and violin, guitar and voice, as well as a *Nouvelle méthode pour la guitarre,* all of which were published.

Another was Antoine Marcel Lemoine (1763-1877), a famous guitar virtuoso who also played the violin, composed, and printed music for guitar solo.

A musician who filled the functions of performer, teacher and composer was B. Vidal, who died in Paris in 1800. He wrote a *Nouvelle méthode,* music for solo guitar and compositions for unusual combinations, such as guitar and cello. His concerto for guitar, two violins and bass belongs in this category.

The matter of unexpected instrumental ensemble brings to mind the name of Jean Benoit Pollet (born c. 1753). His *Nocturne* was scored for harp, guitar and flute. Pollet's son, L. M. Pollet (1783-1830), was a virtuoso performer on the guitar.

Once again we are able to name a woman who achieved some fame as a guitarist. The Countess Felicité Genlis (1746-1830), governess to King Louis Philippe, was a noted harpist and guitarist. She wrote pieces for the guitar which remain in manuscript.

Perhaps the most outstanding figure in the history of the guitar in eighteenth century France is Charles Doisy, (d. 1807) who, like Vidal, was not only a composer, teacher and performer, but also an instrument dealer in Paris as well.

He played both the five and six-string guitars and wrote a treatise, *Principes généraux...* for both instruments. A remarkably prolific composer, he left about two hundred works for solo guitar, guitar and piano, guitar and strings, and, strange as it seems, guitar and brass instruments. He wrote no less than fifty variations on the popular *Folia d'Espagna* for solo guitar. This theme was so well-known throughout Europe that it was used as a setting for guitar compositions by many guitarists and was referred to by Robert de Visée in the preface to his first book of guitar music published in France (1682). Here is his amusing statement:

"I have found a new chord [i.e., tuning] on which I have composed a suite of pieces; I hope that the novelty will make them successful. The others — there is no point in distinguishing them by particular names. They will simply be called suites. One will not find any more Folies d'Espagna. There are so many of them in fashion from which all concerts resound that I could only repeat the follies of others."

The Italians, too, seem to have been captivated by the *Folia d'Espagna.* Among many Italian masters who wrote variations on this theme were Arcangelo Corelli and Alessandro Scarlatti.

The developments taking place in the various countries of Europe were reflected rather faintly in Spain. The number of Spanish guitarists, composers, and guitar makers was less formidable in comparison to what it had been in the previous century and what it was to be in the following centuries. Nevertheless, significant progress was made in the art of guitar making. The developments in this particular area comprise some of Spain's most important contributions to the history of the instrument.

Probably because in the preceding centuries the guitar had been overshadowed by the *vihuela,* the Spanish school of guitar making did not begin to flourish until the end of the eighteenth century. By this time, it had acquired two of its most important exponents, José and Juan Pages, whose workshop was active from c. 1790 to 1819 in Cadiz, a center for the construction of musical instruments. Their fine workmanship is evident on a guitar made by Juan Pages in 1792. *(Plate LXXXI)* The maker's name, together with the date and the name of the province, can be seen inside the soundbox. Its six double strings represent a transition between the five double string guitar and the six single string guitar.

Obviously the Pages did not start the new Spanish school; they were simply its most important exponents in the late eighteenth century. Two of their teachers, José Benedict and Francisco Sanguino, had exerted considerable influence in the evolution of the modern guitar. An unusual instrument by the latter, built in Seville in 1759, has features that are rarely if ever encountered. Its neck is two and a half times shorter than the soundbox, and the depth of this is almost equal to the length of the neck. *(Color Plate (LXXIX)* The instrument has eight single strings and the fingerboard has only eight frets. Sanguino lavished much care on this guitar as is indicated by the delicate mother-of-pearl inlay.

Juan Matabosch, who worked in Barcelona, counts among the important guitar makers in late eighteenth

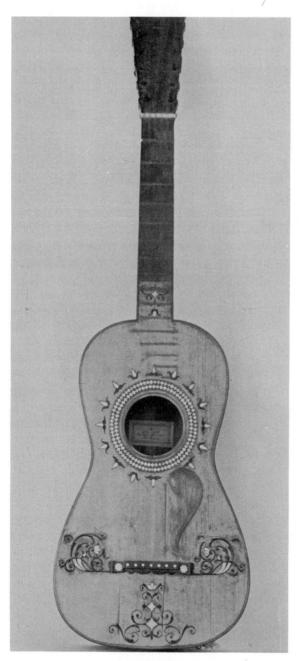

PLATE LXXXI
GUITAR MADE BY JUAN PAGES
1792

century Spain. Like many people associated with the guitar, he originally came from Catalonia and was therefore called "El Catalán," a name given him by Dionisio Aguado. Matabosch's mastery of his craft is apparent from Fernando Sor's first guitar built by Matabosch.

Along with the fine instruments from the workshops of master craftsmen, there exist two anonymous guitars which represent the mediocre builders of the time. *(Plates LXXXII a & b)* One has five double strings and various heraldic insignia such as two *lions rampant* decorating the soundboard. The other has what appears to be a deliberately incorrectly proportioned soundbox. Its sound hole is elaborately carved but the workmanship and the design are commonplace to say the least. The two motifs, one below the bridge and the other at the bottom of the neck, show sufficient similarity to the corresponding motifs on the other anonymous instrument to suggest the same province, if not the same workshop, for both guitars. These instruments may be regarded as feeble attempts by provincial craftsmen to imitate the achievements of their more accomplished colleagues.

In the realm of performance and composition, the dearth of material has limited us to the following names:

Santiago de Murcia was one of the most important guitarists of eighteenth century Spain and one of the last composers to employ tablature. He taught the guitar to Queen Maria Luisa Gabriela of Savoy, the first wife of King Philip V. His *Resumen de acompañar la parte con la guitarra* was published in Madrid in 1714.

Fernando Ferandière enjoyed a high rank as guitarist in the eighteenth century and was spoken of in glowing terms by Aguado. After studying composition at Zamora, this remarkably prolific composer wrote two hundred and thirty-five works which were published in Cadiz and Madrid from 1785 to 1799. Fifty-five of these are for solo guitar and for combinations composed for guitar, violin and flute. The rest include forty trios for guitar, violin and bass; forty quartets for guitar, violin, viola and bass; eighteen quintets, and six concertos for guitar and orchestra. Ferandière's most important contribution, however, was his *Arte de tocar la guitarra española por musica,* a method in modern notation for the six-string guitar, published in Madrid in 1799. A second edition of this work was issued in 1816.

Appearing almost simultaneously with the work by Ferandière was another method entitled *Principios para*

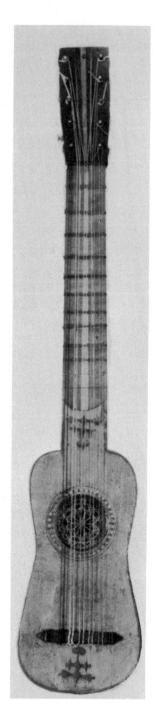

PLATE LXXXII
TWO ANONYMOUS GUITARS. SPANISH SCHOOL

18TH CENTURY

tocar la guitarra de seis ordenes by Don Federico Moretti, a composer of Italian origin. The work was published in 1799, also in Madrid. This two-part method was later translated into Italian and was published in Naples in 1804. Moretti's method established the fundamental principles of modern guitar technique and formed the basis for further development. Moretti was highly praised by F. Sor and Aguado for his work and innovations.

Later in the century, between 1740 and 1760, Antonio Guerrero, a guitarist and writer of *tonadillas* (a type of short Spanish comic opera), performed and composed in Madrid. One of his contemporaries, Guillermo Bates, composed the opera *Pharnaces* in 1756 and wrote *Eighteen Duettinos* for two guitars, two French horns, or two clarinets. These were published in London.

The love of the Spaniards for the guitar was made apparent by the frequency of its appearance in the works of artists such as Francisco Goya (1746-1828). *Bravíssimo,* one of Goya's etchings, attracts attention both for its depiction of the guitar and for its backward glance at age-old themes. The monkey playing the guitar while serenading a huge ass, as shown by Goya, echoes the works of artists in ancient Sumer in which donkeys play lyres. The etching also calls to mind the menageries of musicians so often used by illuminators of medieval scripts.

Other works of art in Spain reflect the waning popularity of the guitar in aristocratic circles and its emergence as Spain's national instrument.

As in Spain, interest in the guitar also declined in Portugal. As a result, many Portuguese guitarists migrated to other countries where their instrument would be regarded with more favor.

Antonio de Costa (1714-1780 or 1790), a priest, guitarist and composer (whom Prat acknowledged as a "great instrumentalist"), traveled to Spain, France, Italy and Austria. Antonio Rodrigo de Menezes concertized in Germany and achieved great fame. Antonio Abreu, a guitarist who was best known for his three-book method, *Escuela para tocar con perfección la guitarra de cinco a seis ordenes,* had this work published in Salamanca in 1799, an auspicious year for guitar methods in Spain.

Predictably, there were few guitar makers in Portugal during this period. Of these, only the names of José Pedeira Coelho and Miguel Ancho have come down to us. These makers did not concentrate exclusively on standard guitars but built the so-called "Portuguese guitars" as well.

Despite its name, the "Portuguese guitar" was not a guitar at all but, like the "English guitar" *(Plate LXXXIII)*, was related more closely to the cittern with six courses of double strings. These instruments were used primarily for accompaniment, although the Italian masters, Geminiani and Giardini wrote serious music for the "English guitar." Both this and its Portuguese counterpart became popular in the eighteenth century and then went out of fashion in the nineteenth.

Italy, despite the slight regression in the popularity of the guitar in the eighteenth century, retained its position as guitar center of Europe by virtue of its contributions to the development of the instrument. Italian composers wrote a

PLATE LXXXIII
FROM LEFT TO RIGHT: ENGLISH GUITAR; FRENCH CITTERN; ENGLISH KEYED CITHER

C. 1800

substantial number of works and, like the guitarists and even guitar makers, traveled widely, bringing to bear on various other countries the influence of their achievements.

Giacomo Merchi (b. 1730) and his brother toured extensively, performing in Frankfurt-Am-Main in 1752 and in Paris in 1753. In 1777 they wrote a method, *Guide des écoliers de guitarre,* after which Giacomo proceeded to England to teach guitar, returning in 1789 to Paris. Both Merchis' composed and, as might be expected, their output includes many duets among a number of *divertimenti* and *barcarolles.*

In 1760 another Italian musician by the name of Marella or Marcella went to England. Two years later a book of duets for five-string guitar written by him was published in that country. His *menuets* and *gavottes,* written in the style of Handel, were considered by his contemporaries to be of high quality.

Of the many Italian composers who wrote for the guitar, the most celebrated was Luigi Boccherini (1743-1805). Like many of his contemporaries, he traveled extensively, performing as cellist with the famous violinist Manfredini. In 1768 these two musicians arrived in Paris where their brilliant playing was warmly received. As a result of this acclaim, they were invited to Madrid by the Spanish Ambassador to France. Although their reception in this city was disappointingly cool, the King's brother, the Infante Don Luis, engaged Boccherini as composer and performer. Later, Boccherini fulfilled similar functions for the King of Prussia, Friedrich Wilhelm II, from whom Boccherini received an annual salary.

Upon the death of Wilhelm, the Marquis de Benavente, a talented Spanish guitarist, became Boccherini's new patron. At this point Boccherini learned to play the guitar and before long his patron began to commission him to write guitar parts into those of his works the Marquis liked best. These compositions led to more commissions. Thus, in 1799, Boccherini composed a *Symphony Concertante* for guitar, violin, oboe, cello and bass.

His most interesting works are the quintets for two violins, guitar, viola and cello, but these met a curious fate. Political problems forced the Marquis to flee from Spain to France where his situation was aggravated by financial difficulties. Having brought Boccherini's quintets with him, and knowing that the composer's name had great drawing power in France, he handed the manuscripts to the Parisian publisher Leduc, who, fearing that the scarcity of good guitarists might lessen the saleability of the music, had the guitar parts transcribed for a second viola. The final outcome was that only three of the guitar quintets were published. Thus the majority of Boccherini's guitar works are now gathering dust in manuscript form. ·

Despite the moments of great popularity that brightened his life, Boccherini died a poor man in Madrid in 1805.

The strides made in Italy towards the improvement of the guitar had an impact on the instrument throughout Europe and other parts of the world, for this century signalled the spread of the instrument in the New World, particularly in South America. Argentina had already produced a number of guitarists. Among them were Manuel Maciel, whose performances took place in 1759, and Antonio Guerrero, who became quite famous.

The Italian craftmens' achievements alone would have earned for their country a lasting place in guitar history. It was through their initiative that the important shift of emphasis — from the elaborately decorative to the more functional and classical style — was effected in guitar construction.

The first steps away from the standards set by Giorgio Sellas and his contemporaries can be seen in a guitar made in Naples in 1790 *(Plate LXXXIVa)* by Antonio Vinaccia, one of twelve-odd members of a famous Neapolitan guitar-making family.

This guitar has inlays around the soundboard and neck as well as ivory decorations on the neck itself; but the preoccupation with greater simplicity is very much in evidence. The six single strings terminate in a tuning head characteristically shaped like a figure 8. A similar style was followed by contemporaries of Vinaccia—the Fabricatores, another important family of instrument makers whose workshop was located in Naples during the years 1770 and 1850.

On a 1797 instrument by Giovanni Battista Fabricatore *(Plate LXXXIV b)*, the inlay is only slightly heavier than it is on the Vinaccia guitar. Instead of ivory, mother-of-pearl was used to decorate the neck. The instrument has six single strings and a tuning head in the shape of a figure 8. As in most eighteenth century guitars, the carved rosette had been replaced by a simple sound hole. The changing attitude towards decoration was accompanied by the development of other interesting features — in this case a slightly longer neck and a greater number of frets which continue into the soundboard.

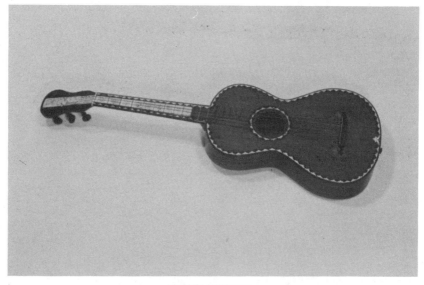

PLATE LXXXIVa
GUITAR MADE BY ANTONIO VINACCIA
1790

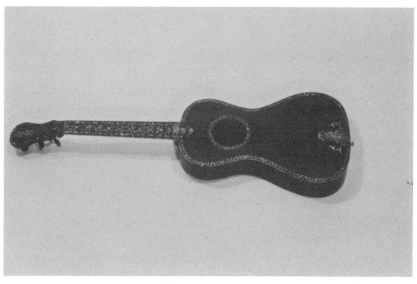

PLATE LXXXIVb
GUITAR MADE BY GIOVANNI BATTISTA FABRICATORE
1797

itar representing a completely different type of con-
on is the little *guitarino* by Carlo Bergonzi, dated
1785. *(Plate LXXXV)* This maker was named after his
grandfather, one of the best pupils of Stradivarius. Bergonzi
took over the Stradivarius workshop in Cremona where
Carlo II, eventually, also established himself. Of his few
surviving guitars, the above *guitarino* is one of the most
interesting. It has six single strings and only seven frets
on the neck. Decoration has been reduced to the barest
minimum: there is only a ring of mother-of-pearl semi-
circles surrounding the rosette.

Bergonzi had considerable influence on the art of guitar
making until his death in 1820. One of his contemporaries,
Trusiano Vincente Panormo, helped to bring the knowledge
of the Italian craft to Paris, Marseilles and London. Born
near Palermo in 1734, Panormo died in London in 1813.

Panormo's son, George Louis, continued to build, in the
words of Fernando Sor, "good-sounding guitars." *(Plate
XCVII)*

Lastly, there was the Italian luthier family of Lorenzo,
Tomaso and Salvatore Carcassi.

SIX-STRING GUITAR

Decidedly the most important factor in the development
of the guitar was the addition of the sixth string. It was
without doubt an innovation that belongs to the eighteenth
century, just as the five-string guitar was a product of the
sixteenth. What may perhaps be open to question is the
Italian origin of the six-string guitar. The evidence, however, favors the following arguments:

The Italian *guitarra battente* of the late seventeenth or
early eighteenth century had an arrangement of six courses
of two strings each. *(Plate LXXXVI)*

The 1732 publication *Neu eröffneter theoretischer und
practischer Music-Saal* by J. F. B. K. Majer gives the tuning
for a six-string guitar and uses Italian tablature for its
musical examples, thereby implying Italian sources for both
music and instrument.

Furthermore, when Jakob August Otto made the first
German six-string guitar, he was said to have proceeded
according to the Italian method.

Thus, just as Italy provided us with the first evidence of
a five-string guitar in the sixteenth century Raimondi engraving, so Italy also seems to have pioneered in the development of the six-string guitar.

The question that may now arise is this: when were
the six double strings replaced by six single strings?

PLATE LXXXV
GUITARINO MADE BY CARLO
BERGONZI. ITALIAN SCHOOL

1785

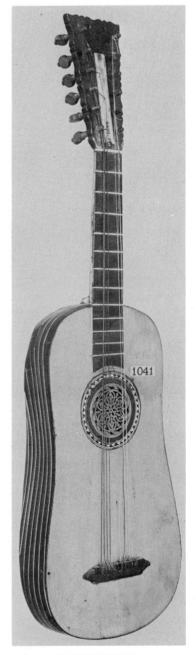

PLATE LXXXVI
GUITARRA BATTENTE. ITALIAN SCHOOL
1700

The precise date is not known but some of the guitars just mentioned provide significant clues.

The guitar by Bernard of Paris *(Plate LXXVII)* has six single pegs on its traditional inverted-guitar-shaped tuning head. This instrument was built in the eighteenth century.

The same characteristics — the six single pegs and similarly shaped tuning head — are present on the guitar by Carlo Bergonzi. *(Plate LXXXV)* This is dated 1785.

The dates on two other six single string guitars are just as explicit: 1790 on the Antonius Vinaccia instrument and 1797 on that of Giovanni B. Fabricatore.

It will, therefore, be safe to assume that the six single-string arrangement goes back to the middle of the eighteenth century. Toward the end of the century, the guitar with six single strings overshadowed all other types. Its arrangement of strings has remained unchanged to the present day.

CHAPTER 7

Unusual Guitars

*T*he historic past, because of its distance from us, often appears as a vast expanse where only monumental events and developments with far-reaching consequences distinguish the landscape. A closer look is needed to bring lesser details into view. Yet, these particulars, like entr'actes, can be charming, amusing, and even enlightening.

The seventeenth century was a period during which the guitar went through any number of structural changes. New and unusual instruments were being fashioned, innovations tried, some of which lasted well into the nineteenth century.

Two main reasons account for the many changes introduced in guitar construction. First, the desire for better sound moved many luthiers to experiment with varying shapes for the instrument. Second, there was at this time a great love for strangeness and novelty for their own sake.

Probably the most spectacular guitars developed in the eighteenth and nineteenth centuries were the closely related lyre-guitar and harp-guitar. *Plate LXXXVII* shows both types. The lyre-guitars are those with the single neck between a pair of wing-like appendages, a feature derived from the Greek lyre of classical art, hence the name "lyre-guitar." In the center of the plate is a "harp-guitar." It has three necks, each with a full complement of six or seven strings. Only one set of strings could be played at a time — unless there were octopuses who played the guitar.

A physicist, mathematician and guitar builder by the name of Josef Petzval specialized in this type of instrument. His first harp-guitar, built in 1862, had two necks, one with thirty-one frets and six strings, the other with twelve frets and six bass strings. The form of these instruments must have served a purely decorative purpose.

A somewhat similar type of guitar, also more or less in the shape of a lyre, was built in England in the early nineteenth century. (*Plate LXXXVIII*) Its three sound-holes have been grouped together under one set of six double strings. The shape of the lyre is suggested by two functionless appendages on either side of the neck.

It was also in England that a guitar with an extended soundbox originated. (*Plate LXXXIX*) The extension is

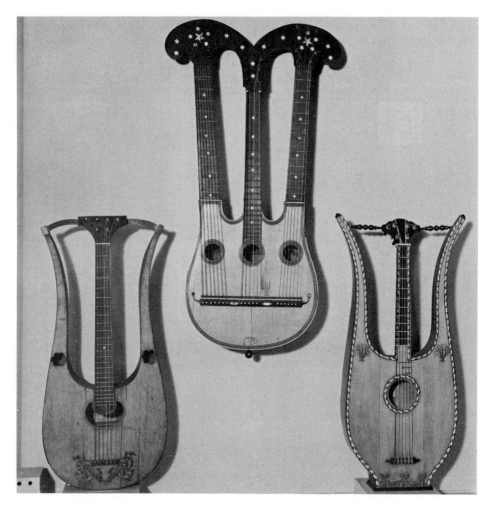

PLATE LXXXVII
FROM LEFT TO RIGHT: FRENCH LYRE-GUITAR; ITALIAN HARP-GUITAR; ITALIAN LYRE-GUITAR

simply a long rectangular protrusion with its own sound hole. This was probably an attempt to improve the sound of the instrument by increasing the resonance of the soundbox.

An interesting collection of miniature guitars showing various types of construction is in the Royal College of Music in London. *(Color Plate XCIV)* These tiny instruments belong to the so-called "Queen's Band" and were given to the college by the late Queen Mary. The collection dates from the seventeenth and eighteenth centuries. The size of these miniature instruments becomes clearly evident when compared with the museum workman's hand in the picture.

PLATE LXXXVIII
ENGLISH LYRE-SHAPED GUITAR WITH SIX DOUBLE STRINGS

PLATE LXXXIX
GUITAR WITH EXTENDED SOUNDBOX

The collection, in addition to guitars, contains two pianos, a cello, a harp, a Chinese "moon-guitar" and two Japanese samisens. We might mention here that an inventory taken of King Henry VIII's collection of musical instruments in 1547 showed that this monarch owned twenty-one real guitars.

Returning to the world of life-size instruments, an unusual and isolated development was taking place in the form of a keyboard being added to the guitar. The resulting keyed guitars had an enclosed apparatus of hammers operated by keys at the low end of the soundbox. To produce sound on a particular string, the corresponding key was simply depressed.

A keyed guitar can be found in the collection of the Metropolitan Museum of Art in New York. A keyed cither, with keys like those used on true guitars, is illustrated on *Plate LXXXIII.* Credit for the invention of this instrument is usually given to the German instrument maker Christian Claus. These keyed guitars were especially in vogue in England.

A slightly more practical attempt to improve the sound of the guitar was made by the Spanish luthier José Porcel, who worked in the latter half of the nineteenth century. He added sympathetic strings to his guitars. These strings were not plucked but were set into sympathetic vibration by the resonance of the guitar.

Plate XC shows such an instrument made by Porcel in 1867. Its nineteen sympathetic strings are set obliquely to the six regular strings and have their own bridge placed perpendicularly to the regular one.

An invention designed to make the upper register of the instrument more accessible was patented in 1828 by a certain A. B. Ventura. In order to do this, the top shoulders of the soundbox were cut in the shape of half moons.

An instrument by a French luthier, Beau of Mirecourt, corresponds precisely to this description. *(Plate XCI)* Beau echoed the half-moon cutout in the design of the tuning head.

A similar type of guitar had a much deeper cutout on only one side of the soundbox, leaving a sharp protrusion. *(Plate XCII)* This feature is present on the modern "jazz-guitar.

Many varieties of guitars being constructed at this time neither followed nor established a trend. One such instrument of this type is shown on *Plate XCIII.* An exhaustive catalog would not be possible here but a few items may

PLATE XC
GUITAR WITH NINETEEN SYMPATHETIC STRINGS
MADE BY JOSÉ PORCEL
1867

PLATE XCI
GUITAR WITH CUTOUT SOUNDBOX
MADE BY BEAU
19TH CENTURY

PLATE XCII
GUITAR WITH CUTOUT SOUNDBOX
19TH CENTURY

be noted.

A guitar made from six thousand separate pieces of wood was built in Guatemala, supposedly by a luthier named Elias Contreras. The instrument was exhibited in Paris in 1888.

An even more unusual guitar, known as a "pedal guitar," was constructed by Eduard Bayer. It rested in proper position on a special table, to one leg of which was attached a pedal. This in turn was connected to a *capo dastro* (bar) on the neck of the instrument. By pressing the pedal with varying degrees of intensity, the bar could be moved from one to four frets at a time, thus transposing the tuning of the guitar into another key.

The novelties in guitar construction were echoed to some extent by novelties in guitar technique. A Viennese guitarist named L. Beilner, whose Opus 1 was published by Diabelli, is said to have used metal extensions to "lengthen" his fingers.

Of all the innovators of the eighteenth and nineteenth centuries, the most famous was J. G. Staufer, whose celebrated *guitarre d'amour* (or *arpeggione*) was played with a bow. Some authorities say that Staufer invented this instrument in 1823, although a certain Peter Teufelsdorfer claimed credit for its invention in the same year. According to him, he played the bowed guitar in the city of Pest in Hungary.

An invention attributed to Staufer with greater certainty is the screw at the base of the guitar's neck which was constructed as a separate unit. By turning the screw the neck could be raised or lowered. In this way the distance between the fingerboard and strings could be adjusted.

Many of these innovations were discarded as soon as they were proven impractical, but three variations on the basic guitar found a certain degree of acceptance.

First was the bass guitar, which consisted of a standard guitar with extra bass strings numbering two to six. These were strung either by having the neck curved to accommodate an extra tuning head as on the Deleplanque guitar previously discussed *(Plate LXXX)* or by adding a second neck without frets. This guitar was known by several names: "bass guitar," "arch-guitar," "double-necked guitar," "theorbo-guitar" and "harp-guitar." It originated in Italy toward the end of the sixteenth century and was used as a solo instrument and in chamber ensembles. Giovanni Battista Granata, as has been noted, composed music for

PLATE XCIII
GUITAR WITH OVAL SOUNDBOX
19TH CENTURY

a five-course guitar with an extra seven bass strings, "Sopra la chittarra Atiorbata." These compositions appear in his book published in Bologna, Italy in 1659.

The other two accepted types of guitar — the *terzguitar* and the *quartguitar* — were closely related to each other. The former was smaller than the modern guitar and was tuned a minor third higher, thus: G-C-F-B♭-D-G. The latter was even smaller and was tuned a fourth (two and a half tones) higher than the modern guitar (A-D-G-C-E-A). Both the *terzguitar* and the *quartguitar* were used in chamber music with the normal size guitar. Many composers, among them Giuliani and Diabelli, wrote for these instruments, Giuliani composing three concerti for *terzguitar* and string orchestra.

These instruments had their direct predecessors. The seventeenth century masters Carlo Calvi and Caliginoso (Foscarini) gave detailed tuning instructions for "small," "middle" and "large" size guitars. As early as the sixteenth century, Luys Milan had written on how to string a smaller size *vihuela* (guitar).

The bass guitar, the *terzguitar* and the *quartguitar,* despite having outlived their other contemporaries, did not survive beyond the first quarter of the twentieth century. Among the unusual guitars they occupied a relatively superior position, but in the context of guitar evolution as a whole their role was a minor though engaging one.

CHAPTER 8

The Nineteenth Century

*T*he various trends taken by the guitar in the preceding centuries can, in retrospect, be viewed as so many roads and byways that led to one destination — the six single-string guitar. The eighteenth century had progressed to this point, but it was not until the nineteenth that the instrument was to reach the peak of its development. By then, the results of experimentation had been evaluated. Technical improvements that could not be adapted to the instrument were soon forgotten or were incorporated in other instruments unrelated to the guitar.

The acceptance of the six single string guitar became universal in the nineteenth century, spreading not only to every part of Europe but to the American continent as well.

Changes in social conditions brought about by the Industrial Revolution contributed to a growing knowledge of the instrument. Improved means of transportation enabled concert artists to travel more widely than they had heretofore. Railways were spreading throughout the continent, and extended concert tours gave many guitarists unprecedented opportunities to perform before large audiences. This was the era of great guitar virtuosi, whose worldwide concertizing helped lay a firm foundation for the instrument's remarkable popularity in the twentieth century.

In the light of these developments, the declining interest in the guitar noted towards the latter part of the eighteenth century may be compared to the lull before a storm. The famous guitarist Simon Molitor (1776-1848) was then emphasizing the disadvantages of the double strings.

These disadvantages included the following: keeping the six double strings in tune throughout the piece, lack in clarity of sound, and the technical problems involved in the performance. The six single string arrangement was then an innovation and as such was still undergoing trial. In addition, there was the problem of notation. Up to now, musicians found it puzzling and difficult to read. This gradually was being replaced by what we know as modern notation. When these transitions were finalized in the nineteenth century, the stability, together with favorable socio-economic conditions, resulted in a remarkable surge of interest in the guitar.

In the first half of the century, the renewed enthusiasm for the instrument was centered in Vienna, hitherto a city that had played but a small role in the history of the guitar. But by this time, Vienna had become a great musical center, attracting many musicians from all over Europe. Guitarists were among those who came to the Austrian capital and their many performances gave the guitar the needed impetus for recognition as a serious medium for artistic expression.

Probably the first important guitarist to settle in Vienna was Simon Molitor, who was born in Neckarsulm, Württemberg in 1766 and died in Vienna in 1848. He came to this city in 1788 to study composition with Abt Vogler. Molitor played the piano and the violin in addition to the guitar. Among his works is a method for guitar, written in collaboration with a colleague by the name of Klingenbrunner.

Molitor's numerous compositions include guitar solos and much chamber music with guitar parts. Among these are trios for violin or flute, viola and guitar, combinations greatly favored by the Viennese masters who were mindful of the frequent contact between famous guitarists, violinists, violists and flutists. Such instrumentalists were integral parts of the rich Viennese musical life of this period.

Younger than Molitor, and working in Vienna at approximately the same time, was Leonhard von Call (1769-1815), born in South Germany. By 1801 he was established as a teacher and performer. In addition, he wrote a great deal of music for guitar which became a source of profit to his publishers because of the popularity it achieved. His guitar music is less difficult technically than many of the demanding compositions of his virtuoso contemporaries and followers. His *oeuvre* included a method for the guitar.

Molitor and Call preceded by a few years the musician

who seems to have had the greatest influence on the formation of the Viennese guitar school. This man was an Italian by the name of Mauro Giuliani (1780-1840?), one of the most important exponents of the guitar and its music in the nineteenth century.

Although he was regarded as a guitar prodigy in his youth, Giuliani's great influence as a performer was felt only after he came to Vienna, in 1807. Following an extended stay in this city, he initiated the trend toward extensive concert tours for guitarists, thus spreading the guitar's acceptance as a serious instrument throughout Europe. He traveled to many countries, his itinerary including cities from London to St. Petersburg, Russia.

In Vienna, Mauro Giuliani's influence on musical life was profound. This we know from descriptions of his various concerts. One of these involved a program of his own compositions including music for guitar and orchestra. The concert was said to have been "rare, lovely and pleasing." These, incidentally, were some of the earliest recitals in which the solo guitarist was the main attraction. Previously the guitarist shared the program with other soloists.

Because of his outstanding technical and musical accomplishments (his playing impressed even Beethoven), Giuliani was on very close terms with many of the most important musical figures of his time. He frequently performed with these artists. A brief account of their activities gives a veritable cross section of Viennese musical life in the first half of the nineteenth century.

Ignaz Moscheles (1794-1870), piano virtuoso and composer from Prague, was one of those with whom Giuliani collaborated successfully. Moscheles himself played the guitar. Shortly after his arrival in Vienna, he and Giuliani (whose popularity was at its peak) gave concerts together playing their own works. One of the favorite items in their repertoire was the *Grand Duo Concertante* for guitar and piano, opus 20, by Moscheles. (As a point of interest, it may be noted that Moscheles was appointed first professor of piano by Mendelssohn at the Conservatorium, founded by Mendelssohn in Leipzig in 1846. Moscheles composed music for a very interesting play by Blangini entitled *The Farewell of the Troubadours*. It was scored for voice, guitar, violin, piano and cello.)

An even more distinguished colleague of Giuliani was Johann Nepomuk Hummel (1778-1837), whose illustrious musical career began with lessons from Mozart. Later, he studied with Albrechtsberger, one of Beethoven's teachers, and Salieri. Hummel was regarded so highly that he succeeded Haydn as conductor of the orchestra of Prince Esterhazy. When Hummel came to Vienna, he became associated with Giuliani, through whom he was introduced to the Viennese guitar world. These associations resulted in Hummel's orchestration of Giuliani's three guitar concertos. The important role of the guitar in many of Hummel's compositions can be attributed to Giuliani.

In 1815 both musicians joined the then famous violinist Mayseder to give six subscriptions, or the so-called "Dukaten," concerts. When Hummel left Vienna his position as pianist in this trio was taken by Moscheles.

Much of Hummel's music is of high quality and his treatment of the guitar is serious and praiseworthy. It is unfortunate that Hummel's music is little known and it is certainly hoped that it will become more accessible to the public.

Giuliani's other associates included Karl Seidler, Spohr, Loder and Anton Diabelli. Though Diabelli (1781-1858) was both a pianist and guitarist, of greater importance was the fact that he was a music publisher. It was in this capacity that his association with Giuliani proved particularly profitable. He issued many guitar compositions, including those of Giuliani, and his efforts to promote guitar music had a significant effect on the increased popularity of the instrument.

Mauro Giuliani had two children, both of whom became prominent in the guitar renaissance, a renaissance given impetus by their father. One, a son named after him, played in concerts with his father. Eventually young Mauro settled as a voice teacher and composer in Florence. The other child was a daughter named Emilia, who is said to have concertized throughout Europe in 1840 and 1841. Emilia was at one time credited with the discovery of harmonics on the guitar.

Neither Molitor, von Call nor Giuliani was born in Vienna; hence, Alois Joseph Wolf (1775-1819) must be cited as the first native member of the Viennese school. As is evident from the above dates, he overlapped the Giuliani period. His wife was a pianist and together the couple appeared frequently in concert.

In contrast to Wolf, whose place in guitar history is relatively obscure, Franz Schubert (1797-1828) is an illustrious figure. This great native Viennese composer played and wrote music for the guitar. Too poor to own a piano, and in fact unable to afford lodgings that could accommodate one, he used the guitar while composing. He wrote many beautiful songs with guitar accompaniment, some of which were published during his lifetime. His most important contribution to guitar literature, however, was the *Quartet* for flute, guitar, viola and cello. It was discovered and published for the first time by G. Kinsky in 1926. The manuscript bears the date February 26, 1814.

Many other Italian guitarists followed Giuliani's example. They concertized and published their music in Vienna. One of the most important of these was Luigi Rinaldo Legnani (1790-1877), who went to that city in 1819. He then traveled to Germany, Switzerland and Italy, giving concerts and developing a technique and virtuosity that were eventually to surpass Giuliani's.

Legnani's interests included guitar construction. Many of his suggestions led to valuable improvements on the instrument and famous guitar makers of the time designed their instruments "after the model of Luigi Legnani." In Ravenna, towards the end of his life, Legnani was known to have spent much time making guitars by hand.

As a composer he was prolific. His works (published in Italy, Austria and Germany) numbered up to opus 250 and included a *concerto, duos, trios, variations, Thirty-six Capriccios* and a most unusual *Scherzo* to be played with only one finger of the left hand.

Another noted Italian guitarist connected with the Viennese school was Matteo Bavilaqua, who published several works in Vienna with the firm of Thade Weigl and that of Diabelli. His *oeuvre* included guitar solos and compositions for guitar and piano, guitar and flute, etc.

The fusion of Viennese and Italian influences was exemplified in the style of the Viennese artist Franz de Paula Stoll (1807- ?). Giuliani and Schulz taught him the guitar and Förster taught him composition. At the age of seventeen, Stoll made his first public appearance; at thirty, he traveled to Germany, France, Holland, Denmark and Russia, playing with various chamber groups and orchestras. In Munich he played with Legnani.

The Viennese school was augmented by members from Germany and Bohemia, many of whom became its significant exponents. Of the Bohemian guitarists, Wenzeslaus Matiegka (1773-1830), was the most important. He arrived in Vienna in 1800 and filled such diverse posts as organist and choirmaster for various churches and as teacher of guitar and piano. His music for the guitar, both solo and for chamber ensemble, includes over thirty compositions, one of which is a trio for the unusual combination of guitar, clarinet and horn.

Among the German guitarists in Vienna was Leonhard Schulz, who played frequently with Franz Mendl, a pupil of Giuliani. Schulz had a son also named Leonhard who made his concert debut as guitarist at the age of eight and, like his father, became a brilliant performer. Another son, Eduard, was an excellent pianist and the three of them traveled through England, Germany and France. They settled in London in 1830 where Makarow, the Russian guitar virtuoso, met the elder Schulz and described him as a man "of large stature, with excellent manners, well-dressed and more English than German looking." His playing, according to Makarow, was characterized by "incredible technique, tenderness, liveliness and, in general, an extremely artful style."

The rest of Europe reflected Vienna's active musical life. Paris and London also resounded with enthusiastic applause for Niccolò Paganini, Mauro Giuliani, Fernando Sor and many others. In London, critics heralded the arrival of nine year old Giulio Regondi, whom they hailed as "another prodigy, an infant Paganini on the guitar!", and the Viennese and Paris press echoed the same sentiments.

Regondi was born in Lyon in 1822. At an early age he began winning honors and applause all over the continent. He grew up to be a very attractive youth of a slim build. It was said that he had rather small hands — which made his virtuosity the more surprising. Through the years he maintained his reputation as a formidable and first-rate guitarist. His instrument was an eight-string guitar built by Staufer of Vienna. In 1841, at the age of nineteen when he was touring Austria with a cellist named Lidel, the Viennese musical journal published an article referring to him:

"His name is Giulio Regondi and he belongs to that classic land where Stradivarius and Amati lived — a land where a genius is not great novelty, but an artist on the guitar as Regondi is, is very seldom found. As a virtuoso he is *more conspicuous* in his mastery of the guitar than was Mauro Giuliani, Legnani, Guglielmi and others heard during the season. . . . It is the soul of melody and he plays the guitar in its purity without any musical tricks."

Regondi died in London in 1872.

The intense activity of the guitarists in Vienna was, not surprisingly, matched and complemented by that of a corresponding Viennese school of guitar makers. Challenged by the developments in guitar technique and the demand for finer instruments, more and more luthiers sought to keep pace with the changing requirements and to produce instruments that would satisfy them. Excellent guitar makers therefore abounded in Vienna at this time. Of these, two may be cited as the most important representatives of the Viennese school.

Johann Georg Staufer (1778-1853), mentioned in the preceding chapter, was an outstanding guitar maker whose workshop was established in Vienna in 1800. Besides being credited with the invention of the *guitarre d'amour* (arpeggione), he also gained a reputation for fine guitars, those built after the "Legnani model" being especially appreciated. Despite Staufer's fame, however, he died in poverty.

Johann Gottfried Scherzer (1843-1870), a famous guitar maker of the old Vienna school, took over the Staufer workshop. He was described as "a little skinny man who always worked alone without help." Experimenting extensively to improve the guitar's tone, and taking advantage of his contacts with physicists to achieve his aim, he became one of the first guitar makers known to have approached his work scientifically, producing as a result fine quality concert guitars.

I had the pleasure of possessing at one time two very beautiful Scherzer instruments, and I must confirm the opinion of others — that the quality of their sound was truly outstanding.

Bohemia at this time also produced a large number of luthiers. Notable was the Lutz family, whose guitars, particularly those made by Anton and Ignaz, were highly prized. Another important craftsman was Josef Urban, who traveled from Vienna to New York and thence to San Francisco, bringing his style of guitar making with him.

The interest in the guitar (which took root in Russia in the mid-eighteenth century during the reign of Empress Elizabeth) blossomed forth in the nineteenth. The popularity of the Italian musicians who introduced the instrument grew in proportion to the increasing popularity of the guitar. With the French musicians of similar accomplishments in Russia, they became firmly entrenched among the nobility, and the influence of the foreigners was such that French became the language of the court. Emperor Paul I is said to have engaged the Italian Carlo Canobbio to teach guitar to three of his daughters. All things French or Italian came to be regarded as superior and desirable.

This cultural and musical climate encouraged the rise of outstanding Russian guitarists. At the same time more guitarists from other countries traveled to Russia. It was not unusual for the Russians to appreciate the foreign guitarists more than their own. This led to a number of native musicians traveling to Italy and France, adopting foreign names and returning to Russia to a musical career enhanced by their new and exotic names.

These attitudes allowed French and Italian guitarists to charge relatively exorbitant sums for lessons and to amass fortunes which allowed them to live like nobles. Attracted by the prestige of these guitarists, more and more Russians began studying the guitar until eventually they rivaled the foreign guitarists in importance as the nineteenth century progressed.

One of these native Russian guitarists was Joseph Kaminsky, who earned a reputation as a teacher. His sonata for guitar with violin obbligato was published in 1799. Like many other Russian guitarists, Kaminsky played the Russian seven-string guitar, tuned in G major thus: D-G-B-d-g-b-d. This unique tuning, while facilitating the plucking of certain chords and allowing for flowing, harp-like arpeggios, made the playing of contrapuntal passages difficult.

The seven-string guitar is still used in Russia and is regarded as a national folk instrument.

The invention of the seven-string Russian guitar has often been attributed to Andreas O. Sichra (1772-1861), one of the giants in the history of the guitar in Russia.

Andreas Sichra was originally a harpist who later adopted the guitar as his main instrument. Although this fact tends to favor the argument that he invented the seven-string Russian guitar, it does not constitute adequate and conclusive proof. His position of prominence, however, is based not so much on the probability of his having invented this instrument as on his other accomplishments. His seventy-five compositions for seven-string guitar became the nucleus of a rich literature for the instrument. He wrote an excellent method for guitar and was the editor of the *Journal pour la guitarre à sept cordes*. This was published in Moscow (1802) and became very popular soon thereafter.

Influenced by his experience as a harpist, Sichra placed great emphasis on the right-hand position:

"We hear the right hand and not the left one. The left hand roams over the frets but the right hand produces the sound, therefore the clarity and articulation [of the tone] depends on the right hand."

In his selfless dedication to teaching, Sichra limited the number of his own concerts despite his being an exemplary performer. He encouraged his pupils to give recitals of their own. Sichra's teaching methods and principles produced many of Russia's fine guitarists.

One of the best of these was Simeon N. Aksenow (1773-1853), who is among those credited with developing the use of harmonics. His compositions include very delightful fantasias on Russian folk melodies.

Another of Sichra's talented pupils was W. I. Swinzow. After his debut in 1825, he became a professional guitarist and concertized with admirable success throughout Russia. He was one of the first seven-string virtuosi to perform in a large public auditorium:

The roster of important Russian guitar virtuosi includes M. T. Wissotzky (1791-1837), a composer and a key figure in a musical and literary group whose members included the distinguished and famous poet Mikhail Y. Lermontov. Wissotzky was most impressive in his ability to improvise. Even Fernando Sor, then visiting in Russia, was highly appreciative of Wissotzky's art.

The preeminence of the seven-string guitar in Russia by no means excluded the six-string type from the country's musical life. Marcus D. Sokolowsky (1818-1883) was one of those who mastered the six-string guitar after having started his musical career as a violinist and cellist. His concert tour during the years 1864 and 1868 took him to Vienna, Paris and London. In London he met Regondi, who highly praised him as a performer. A sensitive man, Sokolowsky was deeply disappointed when his offer to form a guitar class in the St. Petersburg Conservatory was refused.

The men we have considered thus far achieved fame for their abilities as performers and teachers. But one of Russia's finest musicians contributed to the history of the guitar, oddly enough, by writing his memoirs. In this work, Nikolai P. Makarow (1810-1890) chronicled his personal impressions of the personalities and musical abilities of the many famous guitarists he had heard at concerts throughout Europe. His interesting comments on Leonard Schulz have already been quoted. Numerous other guitarists mentioned in this informative volume include Johann Mertz, Matteo Carcassi, Napoleon Coste and Zani de Ferranti.

Equal in importance to Makarow's commentaries were

his own activities in the interests of the guitar. In 1856, he organized in Brussels a competition for the best guitar composition and the best made guitar. The first and second prizes for composition were won by Napoleon Coste and Johann Mertz respectively. The first prize for best made guitar went to Johann Scherzer of Vienna, the second prize to Ivan F. Archusen of Russia. These competitions were part of Makarow's attempts to offset a temporary decline in the guitar's popularity brought about by the death of Fernando Sor and Mauro Giuliani. Towards the same aim, Makarow, himself a fine guitarist, added his own concert performances.

The important guitarists from Western Europe who included Russia in their concert itineraries greatly enhanced the musical life of that country. Zani de Ferranti arrived in 1821 and performed in St. Petersburg. Mauro Giuliani came the following year.

In 1823, the celebrated French ballerina Madame Hullin Sor, wife of the famous guitarist Fernando Sor, came to Moscow in response to an invitation to dance there. Her performances included several ballets to music written by her husband. These circumstances led to Sor's visiting Russia himself. He played a number of concerts which impressed his Russian colleagues greatly and which prompted Sichra and Wissotzky to compose variations on Sor's music. In memory of his Russian visit, Sor composed a guitar duet entitled *Souvenir de Russie.*

In 1829, Peter Simon, a blind court guitarist to the king of The Netherlands, visited Russia and played many recitals. He has been described as "an extraordinary virtuoso."

The visits of the most famous and accomplished guitar virtuosi of that period indicate the importance of Russia in the guitar world at that time.

All this musical activity was complemented by the work of various Russian instrument makers. Ivan Jakowlewitch Krasnostchekow (1798-1875) was an acknowledged master in this field. He won first prize at an exhibition at the Moscow Technical College. The few surviving six and seven-string guitars for which he became famous are now carefully sought by collectors.

Dubrowin, F. Paserbski and S. F. Surow were also nineteenth century Russian guitar makers whose names should be remembered.

The role of the Italians in the Viennese and Russian schools of guitar playing was a formative one. Russia and Vienna, where interest in the guitar was just beginning to manifest itself prior to the nineteenth century, had needed a strong impetus and more extensive exposure to the instrument, and the Italians provided this in good measure. Their proficiency and excellence were, in fact, such that their influence was felt not only in these two countries but in other parts of Europe and the Americas as well. The Italian virtuosi were heard everywhere and there were so many of them that only a whole volume, if not more, could do them justice. We have chosen but a few masters, without whom a history of the guitar would not be complete.

Fernando Carulli was born in Naples on February 10, 1770; he died in Paris in 1841. At first a cellist, he later dedicated himself exclusively to the guitar and became one of Italy's most accomplished virtuosi on this instrument. In Paris, he made a name for himself playing salon recitals, writing his three hundred and sixty compositions, and a method which is still available. He met the guitar maker Lacôte and the two became close friends.

It was common practice at that time for guitarists to frequent instrument makers' workshops and to use these as social headquarters where they could play for each other and criticize their hosts' instruments. Carulli, in his visits to Lacôte's shop, made various suggestions for the improvement of the guitar.

As a teacher, Carulli produced many fine guitarists. Perhaps his most celebrated pupil was Filippo Gragnani (1767-1812), who became one of the first nineteenth century masters to emphasize the suitability of the guitar to chamber music ensemble. Some instrumental combinations for which he wrote are quite unusual. For instance, one of his quartets was scored for violin, clarinet and two guitars.

Carulli continued to perform up to an advanced age and his recitals helped make Paris a formidable center of guitar activity. In time, the brilliance of his playing dimmed and the adulation of the public shifted to a new arrival, the great virtuoso Matteo Carcassi (1792-1853). Understandably, Carulli did not take too kindly to his younger colleague. But Carcassi had come to Paris with successful recitals in Germany, Italy and England behind him. His merits, therefore, could not be denied and it was inevitable that his manner of playing should replace Carulli's in popularity. Today, although Carcassi's approach to guitar technique is no longer considered adequate, his method and studies are still used by many lovers of the instrument.

The Italian masters we have thus far discussed devoted their energies entirely to the guitar; in this lay their greatest contribution to the propagation of its music. There was one, however, who although best known as a violinist, became an important figure in the history of the guitar.

Niccolò Paganini's violin virtuosity has become almost legendary. On it rests his claim to prominence and for it he is best remembered. His other accomplishments are, on the one hand, eclipsed by this virtuosity and on the other they are enhanced by the prestige that was Paganini's on account of it.

Paganini (1782-1840) played and also composed for the guitar. Perhaps his interest in the instrument was aroused by Alessandro Rolla, one of his violin teachers who was also a guitarist and composer for the instrument. During Paganini's violin lessons, Rolla accompanied his young pupil's playing with the guitar. Eventually Paganini applied himself to studying the guitar and composing for it, particularly between 1801 and 1805 when he temporarily retired from the concert stage. During these years, he wrote a substantial amount of music for the solo guitar and guitar with other instruments. Much of this music remains in manuscript.

The number of compositions left by Paganini consists of one hundred forty small solo pieces, a number of sonatas for violin and guitar, quartets for violin, viola, cello and guitar, trios for guitar and two bowed strings.

In general, the guitar parts in much of the chamber music are elementary, but in other works, notably in the Quartets number 7 and 15, as well as in some of the solos, a highly developed technique is required of the performer. Apparently the easy works were intended by Paganini for publication and with a view to making them accessible to a larger number of amateur guitarists. The more difficult pieces were undoubtedly meant for his own use. If his ability as a guitarist can be judged by the difficulty of his music, we must conclude that he was an accomplished performer and possessed an outstanding technique.

Paganini's interest in the guitar brought him in contact with many of the most important figures in the guitar world, among whom were Zani de Ferranti and Legnani. With the latter he played a concert in Turin.

At this point we might direct the reader's attention to an instrument made in the workshop of Grobert (c. 1794-1869), a luthier who worked at the famous instrument center Mirecourt, in France. This guitar was played by

Paganini and Berlioz, both of whose signatures are inscribed on the bare wood in ink on either side of the bridge. *(Plate XCVI)*

J. B. Vuillaume, the great violin maker, loaned the instrument to Paganini to use during his stay in Paris. Paganini returned it with his autograph and Vuillaume then presented it to Berlioz, who was known to be an ardent admirer both of the instrument and of the violinist. Berlioz later added his own autograph and presented the guitar to the museum of the Conservatoire National de Musique in Paris while he was its curator. The guitar remains a possession of the museum to the present day.

Paganini's celebrated pupil Ernesto Camillo Sivori (1815-1894) followed in the footsteps of his teacher by mastering both the violin and the guitar. Although there is no evidence that Paganini gave this student guitar lessons, Sivori somehow became a fine guitarist and his distinguished violin teacher dedicated several works for violin and guitar to "the valiant lad Camillo Sivori." Together, teacher and pupil played these pieces, each taking the violin and guitar parts alternately.

Subsequently Sivori concertized all over Europe and then traveled to the United States in 1846 with the great Italian guitar virtuoso Zani de Ferranti. These two musicians performed in the United States until Zani de Ferranti returned to Europe. Sivori remained in the New World and extended his tour to include Mexico and South America. In 1850, he returned to Italy.

Zani de Ferranti (1800-1878) studied the violin early in his life after having been inspired by the playing of Paganini. In time, he gave up the violin for the guitar.

As a guitarist, he developed into what Paganini (after hearing him play) described as "one of the greatest guitar virtuosi." He also earned Berlioz' praise for his virtuosity and singing tone. Berlioz referred to Zani de Ferranti in his well-known treatise on orchestration: "I repeat that, without being able to play the guitar, one can hardly write for it, pieces in several parts containing passages demanding all the resources of the instrument. In order to have an idea of what the best performers are able to produce in this way, the compositions of such celebrated guitar players as Zani de Ferranti, Huerta, Sor, etc., should be studied."

Zani de Ferranti traveled more extensively than most performers of the day, going to St. Petersburg, Hamburg, Paris, Brussels, London and finally to America as mentioned above. He had the distinction of being one of the

PLATE XCVI
GUITAR MADE BY GROBERT
19TH CENTURY

earliest acknowledged guitar virtuosi to tour the United States. After his American tour, Zani de Ferranti settled in Brussels where he was appointed professor of Italian in the Conservatory there, and where he also became guitarist for the Royal Court. He contributed several solo guitar compositions to the repertoire. These works include *fantasias, nocturnes* and various other pieces.

The intense activity in the area of performance was matched by the efforts of instrument makers to produce not only more but better guitars. Among the many important guitar makers of the time, several of the best were members of the Fabricatore family. We have previously noted an eighteenth century guitar made by Giovanni Battista Fabricatore. His pupil Gennaro Fabricatore worked in the first half of the nineteenth century and his work may be considered representative of the earlier nineteenth century style. This style led a step closer to the modern form that was to be developed later in the century.

Besides those musicians whose primary concern was the guitar, there were several distinguished composers who showed interest in the instrument by participating in matters involving the guitar. Three of the most eminent were Camille Saint-Saëns (1835-1921), Charles Gounod (1818-1893) and Hector Berlioz (1803-1869). The three men, incidentally, were close friends.

Saint-Saëns is known to have owned a guitar and to have at one time been president of *L'Estudiantina,* a musical society dedicated to the mandolin and the guitar. Gounod, according to Prat, wrote a *passacaille* for the Catalonian guitar virtuoso Jaime Bosch-Renard (1826-1895), who settled in Paris and became a very popular guitar teacher. Bosch-Renard wrote many compositions for guitar and a method for learning to play the instrument. He was referred to as "King of the guitar" (Rey de la Guitarra).

Of this group, the most significant was Hector Berlioz. He knew every instrument in the orchestra. The only one he played, however, was the guitar. At one time he earned his living by teaching it.

In his *Treatise on Modern Instrumentation and Orchestration,* Berlioz has a section on the guitar in which he gives instructions for playing the instrument, comments on guitar tuning and gives several examples of arpeggios and chords which can be played on the instrument. Judging from his application of the word "difficult" to chords which are really fairly easy to play, Berlioz had not developed a particularly advanced technique for the instrument. He does, however, show an uncommon understanding of certain problems inherent in guitar composition. The following passage is an indication:

"It is almost impossible to write well for the guitar without being a player on the instrument. The majority of composers who employ it are, however, far from knowing its powers; and therefore they frequently give it things to play of excessive difficulty, little sonority and small effect."

This statement is still relevant today when many composers who are not themselves guitarists write difficult guitar pieces which are very awkward to play.

Berlioz' sensitivity to the beautiful sounds which the guitar is capable of producing may be gleaned from the following quotation:

"Its melancholy and dreamy character might more frequently be made available; it has a real charm of its own, and there would be no impossibility in so writing for it as to make this manifest."

Berlioz composed études for the guitar; these were published in Paris by Aulagnier. Undoubtedly Berlioz helped to raise the guitar's prestige as an instrument just as Paganini had done shortly before him.

Contemporaries of Berlioz included a number of influential French guitarists who also composed for the instrument. One of the most outstanding among these was Antoine L'Hoyer, who lived in Paris in the beginning of the century. He was previously a guitarist to Prince Heinrich of Prussia. His compositions include a concerto for guitar with string quartet, sonatas for guitar and violin obbligato, pieces for two, three and four guitars.

Even opera composers found a place for the guitar in their works. Giuseppe Verdi (1813-1901) in *Il Trovatore* wrote the accompaniment to a troubadour's song for guitar. Again, in *Falstaff* the guitar is given a part. Gioacchino Rossini (1792-1868), his interest in the guitar having been aroused by the playing of Paganini and Zani de Ferranti, used the instrument in *Aureliano* as accompaniment to the Serenade of Almaviva. The guitar found its way in a number of other operas by Rossini, who also wrote a Quintet for guitar and strings.

Later in the century a significant figure appeared in the person of Napoleon Coste (1806-1883). Establishing himself in Paris in 1830 where he associated with important guitarists like Aguado, Sor, Carcassi and Carulli, he performed publicly until 1863 when an accident incapacitated

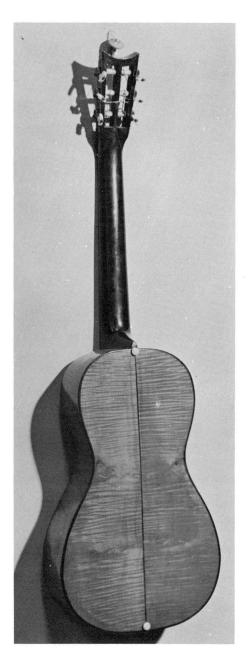

PLATE XCVII
GUITAR MADE BY GEORGE LOUIS PANORMO
1832

his right hand. His musical compositions for the guitar number about fifty and he was one of the first guitarists to attempt a transcription of seventeenth century music into modern notation. Indeed, his most important contribution lay in the impetus he gave to the rebirth of interest in baroque guitar music.

In the previous section on Carulli, we had noted the presence in Paris of the outstanding luthier René François Lacôte, who came from Mirecourt to Paris to become one of the most prominent guitar makers of the century. His association with many important guitarists of the time enabled him to profit from their valuable suggestions for the improvement of the instrument. For Ferdinand Sor, he constructed a guitar with one extra bass string. Taking one of Carulli's ideas, he built a guitar with four extra bass strings.

Another notable French guitar maker was Bloise Mast, member of a family of instrument makers. One of his guitars *(Plate XCVIII)* shows exquisite craftsmanship and a great attention to details of construction.

As already mentioned, guitar makers in France also experimented with unusual forms. The Mauchant brothers of Mirecourt built a guitar with two C-holes framing the usual round rosette. *(Color Plate XCV)* These were perhaps copied from the C-holes of violas as opposed to the F-holes of violins. Other unusual features of this guitar are the soundboard, which curves upward as on the violin, and the double bridge, which is identical to that of the Har-Mosĕ type instrument from Egypt dating back to the second millenium B.C.

While the most salient aspect of the nineteenth century was the great number of traveling virtuosi, the use of the guitar in chamber music also became more pronounced at this time. The masters of the Viennese and German schools particularly seemed intrigued with the idea of combining the haunting, plucked string sound with the timbres of other instruments. Thus, besides the common guitar-viola-flute trio, we find ensemble combinations such as the following: quartets for flute, strings and guitar; flute and guitar; violin and guitar; two flutes, guitar and cello; piano and guitar, etc.

Among the composers who produced such works were Johann Bayer (1822-1908), Joseph Küffner (1776-1856), Johann Kapeller and Johann Kaspar Mertz (1806-1856). Mertz was the most interesting of the group. He used an eight-string guitar and later the ten-string type. He was

PLATE XCVIII
GUITAR MADE BY BLOISE MAST

strongly attached to the Viennese school, over which he had some influence. The Russian virtuoso Makarow, hearing Mertz in Vienna, had words of high praise and some of criticism for his playing. In his book, Makarow wrote that Mertz plucked the bass strings too harshly, a fault which Makarow regarded as typical of the German school.

Wherever the guitar became popular, it attracted the attention of prominent composers who then composed for it. Germany was no exception. Carl Maria von Weber (1786-1826) played the instrument and used the guitar in his chamber music compositions. His comic opera *Abu Hassan* (1811) makes use of two guitars, and his compositions for voice and guitar are very ingratiating.

It might seem surprising that a composer of monumental music dramas, who did not hesitate to call for two hundred piece orchestras, should have considered the guitar useful at all, but Richard Wagner (1813-1883) was known to have turned often to it as an aid while composing. For the recitatives of Lucia and Helden in the melodrama *Enzio,* he wrote guitar accompaniment, as also for the Serenade of Beckmesser in *Die Meistersinger.* (This Serenade is often called *Fugue with Chorale,* and is written in the style of Bach.)

Niels Wilhelm Gade (1817-1890) was a Danish composer from Copenhagen whose interest in the guitar (which he played quite well) was natural since his father and uncle, Sören and J. N. Gade respectively, were known guitar makers.

The increasing use of the guitar in the nineteenth century gathered so much momentum that the instrument eventually become known in areas of Europe where it was unknown before this time. The island of Corsica, for example, produced Jacques Tessarech (1862-1929), a civil engineer by profession who later sacrificed his career, moved to Paris and dedicated his life to the study of the guitar. He became an accomplished performer but, unable to perform publicly due to nervousness and shyness, his contribution was that of adding to the guitar's literature. Among his works are: *Treatise on the Guitar and its Technique* (Paris, 1904); *The Evolution of the Guitar* (Paris, 1924), containing fifty pages of music, and *The Polyphonic Guitar.* Late in his life, he was appointed professor of the guitar at the Nice Conservatoire.

In Greece, the guitar made such inroads that several guitar makers established themselves in Athens. Georgios K. Evangelides (1860-?), a native of Cyprus (who modeled his guitars after French instruments), and Jorge Makropulos, who worked in Athens from 1865 to 1890, were two of these.

Perhaps a salient development in the nineteenth century was one that might be termed the Renaissance of the guitar in England. During the Restoration period and early in the evolution of the instrument, this country had played a central role; one, however, which it did not maintain. The frequent references to the "guitar" in the eighteenth century involved, with few exceptions, the so-called "English guitar." This, as we have seen, was not related to the guitar. When London became, in the nineteenth century, a musical center equal in importance to Paris, Vienna and St. Petersburg, it attracted a large number of guitarists who came to perform and participate in the stimulating musical life. Virtually all the guitarists discussed in the preceding pages played in London. The many recitals given by traveling virtuosi gave the English a wide exposure to guitar music, thus reviving and intensifying the people's interest in the instrument.

Many of these guitarists moved on from England to other countries but several remained to teach and perform. One of the most influential of these was the German-born musician Ferdinand Pelzer (1801-1860). Settling in London in the first half of the century, he was soon in great demand as a teacher and performer. He performed successfully with distinguished artists such as Moscheles and the famous flutist Dressler. Pelzer involved himself also in publication, issuing a guitar magazine called *The Giulianiad,* in honor of Giuliani. These activities exemplified those which solidified the foundation for the growth of interest in the guitar in England.

Pelzer's work was continued by his daughter Catherina Josepha, for whom he had ordered a special pair of instruments from Lacôte. After a successful career as a child prodigy, Josepha married and became known as Madame Sidney-Pratten. She was extremely active as a teacher. Two of her numerous students were F. A. Cramer and his friend Ernest Shand (1868-1924), who wrote over two hundred works, many of which were for guitar.

Predictably, luthiers thrived in England at this time. One of these was George Louis Panormo, son of the noted luthier, Trusiano Vicenzo Panormo (1734-1813), who settled in London in 1772. George Louis was born in London in 1774 and died there after 1842. One of his guitars made in 1832 *(Plate XCVII)* shows striking similarities to the French instrument by Bloise Mast. *(Plate XCVIII)*

In addition to George Louis Panormo's distinction as an English luthier, he is also known as the father-in-law of one of Spain's outstanding virtuosi, Don A. F. Huerta y Katurla (1804-1875).

The interesting career of Huerta began when, as a young man, he left military school and went to France where he distinguished himself as a guitarist and teacher. He then went to the United States to concertize in 1825-26, some twenty years before Zani de Ferranti. Huerta was thus the very first guitarist, to my knowledge, who toured the United States. In 1827, he returned to London where he played with the pianist Moscheles, the violinist De Bériot, and the harpist Labarre. Subsequently, he went to Paris where he was welcomed and highly praised by Lamartine, Victor Hugo, Fétis and other famous men. Rossini counted Huerta among his intimate friends.

In 1833, Huerta left Paris for Spain where he became guitarist to Isabel II and was made a Knight of the Order of Gregory the Great and of the Order of Carlos III. From Spain, he traveled to Malta, Constantinople, Egypt and the Holy Land. Here, then, is an example of a concert guitarist who, almost one hundred and forty years ago, practically circled the globe to concertize.

It is unfortunate that Huerta's playing could not have been recorded for future generations. His virtuosity and mastery of the guitar is clearly indicated by Berlioz' opinion of his artistry. In the *Treatise on Orchestration,* Berlioz described Huerta, with Zani de Ferranti and Fernando Sor, as one of the three most outstanding guitarists of that time.

The success of Huerta in London, Paris, the United States and other countries illustrates a curious paradox. Spain produced many outstanding virtuosi at this time and it is unquestionable that guitar music flourished in nineteenth century Spain. Yet the Spanish guitar virtuosi and the Spanish exponents of the instrument, like Huerta, achieved their greatest successes outside their native country. Fernando Sor, probably the most important Spanish virtuoso of the century, exemplified these emigrant guitarists, although his reasons for leaving his homeland may have differed from those of his compatriots.

Fernando Sor was born in Barcelona in 1778 and he died in Paris in 1839. This man (whose renown was based largely on his being a representative of the venerable traditions of the guitar in Catalonia) began his career as a composer of operas, ballets, oratorios and other forms of orchestral music. While in Madrid, he enlisted in the French army and eventually achieved the rank of captain. When Napoleon's power disintegrated in Spain in 1813, Sor was compelled to flee to Paris. There he came in contact with the composers Méhul and Cherubini who, upon hearing him play the guitar, persuaded him to give recitals. Pursuing his career as guitarist, Sor went to London and then to Russia. In this latter country he was regarded as a Frenchman, so closely associated had he become with his adopted country. Following a second trip to London, Sor settled permanently in Paris in 1828. By this time he was recognized universally as one of the most significant masters of the guitar, a distinction accorded him presently.

Sor was the only guitarist of his time to perform at the Royal Philharmonic concerts in London. He also collaborated with the guitar makers Lacôte and Panormo, both of whom respected and adopted many of his suggestions. As a composer, he wrote some of the finest guitar compositions of the nineteenth century. Besides his sonatas, fantasias and other extended pieces, his delightful studies remain favorite items in the repertoire of many guitarists today.

Closely associated with Sor, although representing a completely different school of guitar playing, was Dionisio Aguado y Garcia (1784-1849), an important virtuoso and composer. Their warm friendship is symbolized by a duet, *Les Deux Amis,* written by Sor for a concert which featured the two. Like Sor, Aguado eventually settled in Paris but returned to Madrid in 1838 because, it is said, of homesickness. He died there in 1849.

Aguado was far from being a prolific composer; he left only a few short pieces and studies. But he was an important pedagogue and his *Metodo para guitarra* (1825) is still considered one of the best methods written in the nineteenth century. It has been translated into other languages and reprinted several times.

In contrast to Sor, Aguado used his fingernails for plucking and employed a hand position which differed considerably from that of Sor. He initiated the use of a stand to support the instrument while playing it in a sitting position. (The German guitarist Bayer is reputed to have employed such a stand to support the guitar while it was played in a standing position.)

Among Aguado's many pupils was Antonio Campo, his favorite. After 1849, this student brought to light his teacher's compositions and published *Gran solo de Sors refundido per Aguado.*

Julian Arcas (1832-1882) was another Spanish guitar virtuoso. He was at the height of his fame between 1860 and 1870. After touring Spain, he traveled to England and performed at the Brighton Pavilion before members of the Royal Family. His playing was highly praised by *The Brighton Guardian.*

Returning to Spain, he continued to concertize and finally settled in his birth place, Almeria. He is said to have been a professor at the Royal Conservatory and Knight of the Royal Order of Carlos III. No less than eighty of his compositions, most of them based on national melodies and dances, have been published.

Probably the most important contribution to pedagogy and guitar technique from Spain is embodied in the works of Francisco Tarrega (1852-1909). These include his compositions, which rank among the best in the late nineteenth century.

Tarrega received his first guitar instruction at the age of eight. This was followed by studies at the Conservatory of Music in Madrid where he later taught guitar. He also taught in the Conservatory of Barcelona and made numerous transcriptions of works by Bach, Handel, Mozart and Schubert. In addition, he wrote many compositions of his own that exhibit the increased complexity of harmony and technique made possible by his new approach to guitar playing.

This new approach, which is still used today with some modifications, involved a major change in the position of the right hand. Instead of being held obliquely to the strings as was common among most of Tarrega's predecessors, the hand was held perpendicular to them. It is conceivable that the technique developed by Tarrega independently was similar to that used by earlier guitarists. The description of the right hand position given by Guerau in the seventeenth century could be interpreted as referring to a similar if not the same technique. However, it was only after Tarrega's demonstration of its actual applicability that the technique became firmly rooted in practice.

Most present day guitarists have modified Tarrega's position from one that held the fingers perpendicular to the strings to one that holds the fingers at a slight angle. This allows the guitarist to pluck the strings with the left side of his fingers, thus producing a better sound.

Tarrega's technique made more convenient the use of

the so-called "supported stroke" or "hammer stroke." This involves resting the plucking finger on the string immediately below that which has been plucked. Although the invention of this stroke is usually attributed to Tarrega, the master himself once told his pupil Emilio Pujol that the stroke was previously used by Julian Arcas for rapid scale passages. The "hammer stroke" was also undoubtedly used by harpists then as it is now. Such a stroke is in fact quite natural on a plucked string instrument. It was probably used many centuries before by the harpists of Egypt. At any rate, Tarrega's accomplishments were definite and significant aids toward the formulation of modern guitar technique. They helped revitalize the popularity of the guitar, which had declined in previous years.

Paralleling Tarrega's achievements were developments in guitar construction. Just as his approach to guitar playing laid the foundation for more advanced practice, so the work of the celebrated guitar maker Antonio Torres Jurado led directly to the basic form of the guitar in which it is now known. He placed great emphasis on the importance of the top soundboard in the production of tone, and he perfected and may even have invented the use of fan-bracing under the soundboard to enrich the sound. He standardized the string length to sixty-five centimeters, the measure still used today. Many details of construction too numerous to be listed here benefited from Torres' methods, and many guitar makers of the twentieth century reflect in their work the great debt owed this innovator.

Torres (1817-1892) was a pupil of the luthier José Pernas, himself a fine craftsman who worked in Granada in 1850. Torres' activity in the field of guitar construction is divided into two periods, separated from each other by a few years during which he was compelled (for financial reasons) to engage in another business. The first period was from 1850 to 1869; the second, from 1880 to 1892. His guitars are classified accordingly.

The earliest example of Torres' work known to the present author dates from 1852. *(Plate XCIXa.)* It is now owned by Senor Joaquin Arcas of Barcelona. But the instrument of most interest to the guitar lover is the one owned by Miguel Llobet, made by Torres in 1859. *(Plate XCIXb.)*

Torres' innovations resulted in the foundation of a true Spanish school of guitar making whose membership eventually included the most important luthiers of the late nineteenth and early twentieth century. One of these was Manuel Ramirez (?-1920), of a distinguished family of

PLATE XCIXb
GUITAR MADE BY ANTONIO TORRES
OWNED BY M. LLOBET
1859

PLATE XCIXa
GUITAR MADE BY ANTONIO TORRES
1852

instrument makers. A number of his instruments bear a similarity to those of Antonio Torres.

The nephew of Ramirez, José, has maintained the family's reputation to the present day.

Among Ramirez' many outstanding pupils, the most distinguished was Enrique Garcia (1868-1922), who, by winning first prize at the 1893 Exposition of Chicago at the age of twenty-five, gave ample indication of his phenomenal talent. Garcia, in turn, had one very gifted pupil, Francisco Simplicio (1874-1932), who carried the tradition of the Spanish school into the twentieth century.

It is therefore evident that Torres and his disciples constituted the most important single factor in the formation of the Spanish school of guitar making in the late nineteenth century. It must not be forgotten, however, that the activity of many unknown luthiers who preceded them contributed to the fruitfulness of later efforts. The general stylistic trends of the previous era continued through the early and middle years of the nineteenth century, in some cases combining them with modern features. Guitars with six double strings continued to be built and designs traced back to the Baroque period and earlier continued to be used. A guitar by Joseph Alcaniz *(Plate Ca)* gives evidence of the adherence to the past and the adoption of the new. Built in 1804, it is also the earliest example of a guitar with nineteen frets, the number now found on modern instruments.

A Guitar by Auguste Altimira *(Plate Cb)* shows a similar combination of old and new. Built in the middle of the nineteenth century, it has such eighteenth century features as inlay work and a modern device, the machine head.

No account of the guitar in the nineteenth century would be complete without a brief survey of the instrument's increasing popularity on the American continent.

, The guitar was known in the New World as early as the sixteenth century when the Spanish colonizers sold *vihuelas* to the Aztec Indians. But it was only in the nineteenth century that the instrument began to have a steadily increasing number of devotees. The coming of Spanish and Portuguese artists undoubtedly did much to encourage this state of affairs and, in South America particularly, their activities led not only to the promotion of the guitar as an instrument for the performance of serious music but also to its entrenchment in the folk music of many countries.

These developments inevitably resulted in an increasing number of known guitarists and guitar makers. We have

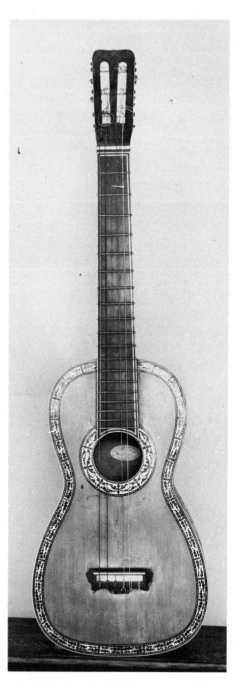

PLATE Ca
GUITAR MADE BY JOSEPH ALCANIZ
1804

PLATE Cb
GUITAR MADE BY AUGUSTE ALTIMIRA

the names of José Esteban Antonio Echeverria Espinosa (1805-1851), a guitarist, poet and sociologist who lived in Buenos Aires, and of his follower, Martin Moreno (1833-1919), from Rosario de Santa Fe, Argentina.

Uruguay produced several guitar makers, two of whom were José Pau and José Del Puerto Romero (1874-1932) of Montevideo. From Guatemala there was Elias Contreras, who built instruments in the second half of the nineteenth century.

Among many guitarists from Brazil Alfredo de Souza-Imenez (1865-1918) may be cited. He had a wide repertoire of guitar music which included transcriptions of Beethoven. He is said to have belonged to the school of Aguado.

From Cuba there was Juan Martin Sabio (1868-1920), whose pupil Severino Lopez became the first teacher of one of our finest contemporary guitarists, Rey de la Torre.

Similar developments took place in the United States. The early interest in the guitar (George Washington ordered English guitar strings for his niece, who played the instrument, and Benjamin Franklin was a serious student of the guitar) blossomed forth in the nineteenth century. From then on the guitar steadily gained recognition in North America.

We have already noted the extensive concert tours of Huerta and Zani de Ferranti, both of whom did much to spark this development. Several other foreign guitarists chose to remain and settle permanently in America, teaching throughout the country. Miguel S. Arrevalo, a musician of Spanish descent, taught in Los Angeles and San Francisco. His pupil Luis T. Romero, also of Spanish descent, came to the United States as an adolescent, taught in Boston and died there in 1893.

Guitar makers who migrated to the New World include Joseph Bohmann, a Bohemian who came in 1873 and built fine guitars in Chicago.

But the most important figures in the pioneering days of the guitar in the United States were native Americans. One of the pioneers was Justin Holland (1818-1887) from Virginia. He published a fine method in 1874.

W. L. Hayden was one of the first to publish sheet music for the guitar in America. This was issued by Oliver Ditson & Co. in 1889-90.

Manuel Y. Ferrer (1828-1904), a guitarist from California, became a virtuoso, regarded during his lifetime as one of America's finest. He transcribed music for guitar and was prolific as a composer. He taught the guitar for half a century. One of his students, Vahdah Olcott Bickford, organized the first guitar society in America.

Charles de Janon was a versatile and highly respected guitarist and composer. Born in Cartagena, Colombia in 1834, he came to New York at the age of six. His compositions and transcriptions for guitar (nearly one-hundred in number) became quite well-known in America and many of them were published in New York and Boston.

Charles James Dorn (1839-1910), a Bostonian by birth, traveled to Germany to receive guitar instruction from his uncle Jacob Dorn, a guitarist and French horn player in Karlsruhe. After obtaining his musical education, Dorn returned to the United States and settled in Boston to teach, compose and concertize.

The traditions established by these guitarists continued into the twentieth century. They were advanced by men like William Foden (1860-1947), who enjoyed a good reputation as performer and was admired particularly for his marvelous tremolo. After touring the United States, he settled in New York to teach. His pupil George C. Krick (1871-1962) became one of America's most distinguished teachers. At one time teacher and pupil appeared jointly in concerts in New York. In 1906, Krick founded a Conservatory of Music in Philadelphia. Later settling in St. Louis, he established what must be a record in the number of years devoted to teaching the guitar — sixty years. His death at the age of ninety caused great sorrow in the guitar world.

A contemporary of William Foden, Cornelius Daniel Schettler (1874-1931) from Salt Lake City, Utah, also adhered to nineteenth century traditions. He went to Germany in 1903, studied the cello, and gave successful guitar concerts. In 1905, he won first place for America in a contest sponsored by the World Guild of Guitar Players in Germany. Returning to Salt Lake, he taught guitar, cello and other string instruments.

Due to the great activity of the guitarists, the public became increasingly aware of the possibilities of the guitar. The interaction between performer and audience resulted in the growth of both. Soon circumstances favored the publication of a magazine devoted primarily to the guitar, its music and its performers. Called *The Cadenza* and issued monthly, it was published by Clarence L. Partee, a guitar teacher from New York. One of its contributors, Philip J. Bone, an Englishman, eventually compiled the biographies of guitarists he had written for *The Cadenza* and published them in book form at the suggestion of Vahdah Olcott Bickford.

Upon the death of Clarence Partee, Walter Jacob, a teacher and arranger from Boston, took over the publication of *The Cadenza.*

Again, the rising popularity of the guitar created a greater demand for instruments. This time the increased demand was met by using machines and factory methods in addition to the traditional handcraft. One of those who founded a factory for large-scale guitar production was Christian Friedrich Martin (1796-1873), a member of a German family of violin makers who came to America in 1833. Martin's establishment is still in existence and thriving today.

To some extent, the events of the nineteenth century — the changes in the instrument, the greater opportunities for performers to travel, the wider distribution of the instrument — may be regarded as natural and predictable parts of an evolutionary process. But the pace and nature of change often verge on the startling. The age old practice of making instruments entirely by hand has been replaced for the first time by machinery capable of mass production. This has shocked some, saddened others and gladdened still others. As with other developments, these changes form the patterns of light and shade peculiar to the picture of the nineteenth century. Many of them were to have an influence on the future course of the guitar's history. They signaled, with a measure both of certainty and uncertainty, the events that were to take place in the twentieth century.

CHAPTER 9

The Twentieth Century

*A*ll histories, particularly those that cover great spans of time, are by necessity partly hypothetical. Many landmarks are obliterated by the sands of time and only theory can create the continuity needed to retrace events and reconstruct epochs. The work of dealing with the present, however, constitutes a problem of a different nature. It involves the problem of objectivity and perspective. The difficulty of being too close to events, perhaps of being a part of them, replaces the difficulty of investigating our subject from a distant past. Only the historian of the future will be able to describe accurately events and personalities deserving a place in history. It is therefore necessary to keep in mind that chronology can in some cases obscure, in others, magnify, and in still others, clarify.

Our century has been and continues to be witness to an unprecedented surge in the acceptance of the guitar as an instrument for serious artistic expression. At no other time in the history of the guitar has it been so welcome on the concert stage. Indeed, many music lovers, confronted with the present phenomenon, have made the pardonable mistake of thinking that the guitar must have been nothing more than a fashionable plaything in previous centuries. It is hoped that the preceding pages have had some effect in refuting such an impression. The guitar's present position of prestige could not have been possible had the foundations not been firmly laid through the centuries.

There are two basic reasons for the tremendous popularity of the guitar today. The first and more obvious one is rooted in phenomena that belong exclusively to the twentieth century. The revolutionary technological progress and the development of mass media communications and faster, more efficient modes of transportation are its more notable aspects. Radio, television, the recording industry, communications satellites, jet travel *et al* have contributed to speedy global exposure of the instrument. Musicians are now able to concertize all over the world in the course of one concert season. They are able to reach huge audiences—not only those actually present at a performance but those who view television, listen to broadcasts and to phonograph recordings. More people are, therefore, drawn into the circle of participants, whether as composers, performers or listeners; more opportunities are created to arouse interest in the guitar.

The second reason, though less dramatic, is not less significant. It is an extension, a natural consequence of the developments that have taken place in past centuries.

It will be recalled that by the end of the nineteenth century, guitar technique had been brought by Tarrega to the point where it was a truly fine art, ready for the next step into what we now know as modern technique. The great guitar makers, most notably Torres, had developed an instrument which, with slight variations, retains to this day the classic form of the guitar. These crucial events simply had to lead to the full realization of the guitar's potential in the twentieth century. Hand in hand with the forces and resources that have emanated from the present, the circumstances inherent in the second reason have led to the great wave of popularity that has swept over the guitar. It is a wave that continues to rise towards its apex.

Tarrega had many outstanding pupils but by far the most important was Miguel Llobet. Born in 1878, he was tragically killed in Barcelona in 1937, the victim of a bomb explosion during the Spanish Civil War.

After studying at the Barcelona Conservatory of Music, Llobet began concertizing throughout Spain. Continuing his travels, he appeared in Paris, England, the United States, South America, Berlin, Munich and Vienna; in short, almost all the important cities in the Western World. Wherever he performed, Llobet was acknowledged a master and he won innumerable music lovers to the cause of the guitar.

Judging from what has been written about him by those who heard him at the height of his powers, as well as from the few recordings he made, we can definitely proclaim him one of the supreme virtuosi of the guitar, possessed of a deep understanding of the instrument, an incredible technique and impeccable musicianship.

Llobet taught a considerable number of outstanding present-day guitarists. Of these, two are important: Maria Luisa Anido (1907-   ), who still concertizes throughout the world, and José Rey de la Torre of Cuba.

Born on December 9, 1917, Rey de la Torre went to Barcelona at the age of fourteen to study guitar with Llobet. Three years later, he played a recital at the Granados Academy in the same city. This was the beginning of a successful career as concert guitarist. It was at his instigation that the young composer Julian Orbon, Rey de la Torre's brilliant countryman, wrote the magnificent "Prelude and Dance" which has been recorded by Rey de la Torre under its original name, "Prelude and Toccata."

The giant of the twentieth century and unmatched virtuoso is Andrés Segovia, a close friend of Miquel Llobet. He continues to astonish the public with his absolute mastery of guitar technique and his wonderful command of tone color.

Born on February 21, 1893, Segovia felt compelled to teach himself the guitar. The technique he eventually developed was an improvement on Tarrega's and one of its most important aspects is precision in all matters, particularly with regard to the right hand. The exceptional technique that he came to possess accounts in large part for his sway over untold numbers of concert goers. He has done perhaps more than any other single performer to attract devotees to the guitar.

Each year, for over half a century, he has concertized throughout the world and he has to his credit innumerable radio and television performances. He has recorded practically his entire repertoire. The golden jubilee of his first concert was commemorated in 1958 with the issuance of a three-record album of guitar music brilliantly performed by the master.

Segovia's involvement with the guitar went beyond performance. He has consistently inspired contemporary composers to write for the instrument. His close relationship with the composer Mario Castelnuovo-Tedesco resulted in the first guitar concerto written in the twentieth century (1939). Castelnuovo-Tedesco has also written for Segovia a quintet for guitar and strings, a sonata, *hommage à Boccherini,* and many other pieces.

Also at the instigation of Segovia, Manuel Ponce of Mexico, Joaquin Rodrigo of Spain and Alexander Tansman of Poland have written for the guitar. Rodrigo and Ponce have composed guitar concerti which have become well-known. Ponce, having already made his name as a composer, has contributed considerably to solo guitar literature. His three sonatas, sonatina and the *Variations sur "Folia de España" et Fugue* are specially noteworthy.

The growing audience for the guitar created by Segovia encouraged many important younger guitarists to give concerts and allowed them to aspire to greater acceptance. One of the most brilliant of these is the young British guitarist and lutenist Julian Bream (1933-   ). Although still in his thirties at the time of this writing, Julian Bream has already established himself as, without doubt, one of the most outstanding guitarists and sensitive musicians of today. Because of his catholic musical taste, he is able to combine within one program compositions as varied as the Dowland lute pieces and the atonal *Quatre Pièces Brèves* by Frank Martin. Bream has also broadcast and recorded frequently and has encouraged important British composers to write for the guitar. The results include Lennox Berkeley's delightful *Sonatina* for guitar, Benjamin Britten's *Chinese Songs* for voice and guitar, and *The Nocturnal after John Dowland* for guitar.

The great possibilities for performing music for two guitars have been demonstrated by the highly gifted guitar duo, the late Ida Presti and Alexander Lagoya. Ida Presti was a child prodigy and in her lifetime ranked as one of the foremost female guitarists. Lagoya, like Presti, combined excellent technique with great musical sensitivity. This husband-and-wife team always exhibited perfect co-ordination, the playing of one balancing and complimenting that of the other.

Besides the transcriptions of Bach's keyboard music which they played so effectively, Ida and Alexander Lagoya performed original compositions for two guitars by early masters. Much music has been written for them by composers such as Joaquin Rodrigo, their fellow Frenchman, D. Lesur, A. Jolivet and Pierre Petit. As a consequence, interest in writing for the hitherto obscure combination of two guitars has been further aroused. Ida and Alexander Lagoya have proven to music lovers throughout the world that two guitars make possible many wonderful and memorable musical experiences.

Ida Presti's untimely death—she was in her early forties

—was a great loss felt deeply not only by this author but by her many friends and devotees throughout the world. April 24, 1967 will always be remembered as a sad day by all who love Ida and the guitar.

The guitarists briefly discussed above represent those who have already carved niches for themselves in guitar history. There are many more in the younger generation who have been performing publicly for a few years and who are on their way towards establishing a substantial reputation. Probably the most important among these is John Williams, a young Australian now living in England. He concertizes frequently throughout the world and has made several splendid recordings.

Needless to say, these young guitarists are indebted to the many dedicated teachers now active in virtually all countries. Many of these are superb performers but they have allowed their concertizing to be curtailed by heavy teaching schedules.

The endless number of fine performers and teachers in the twentieth century is matched by further developments in guitar construction. The monumental achievements of the Spanish school are perpetuated in the guitars of Santos Hernandez (1873-?) and José Ramirez de Calarreta (1885-   ). A prominent German luthier of the twentieth century was one Hermann Hauser (1882-1952), whose fine instruments are used by many of today's concert guitarists. The family tradition is continued by his son Hermann Hauser, Jr.

There are so many fine contemporary guitar makers that we can only mention a few.

France may well take pride in the work of Robert Bouchet, Spain in the work of Ignacio Fleta and the United States in that of Manuel Velazquez.

The traditions of the past in guitar construction have been respected and altered in the interests of better instruments. Technology and innovation are responsible for the adoption of nylon strings to replace the old ones made of gut. This has practically revolutionized guitar playing. Because the new strings are much stronger, require less frequent tuning and produce better sound, they are more practical and more desirable, particularly for concert performance. They were first tried on the stage by the Brazilian singer-guitarist Olga Coelho in January, 1944 in New York. Today, it is standard practice to use nylon strings for the first three strings of the guitar, and nylon spun with metal for the three bass strings.

Scholarship has been enhanced in the twentieth century by musicological research on the guitar. Philip J. Bone (1873-1964) of England, Josef Zuth (1879-1932) of Germany (who, incidentally, was the teacher of the Austrian guitarist Luise Walker) and Domingo Prat (1866-1944) of Spain and Argentina have each written a comprehensive dictionary of guitarists, guitar makers and composers. The contributions of men such as these have thrown much light on many aspects of guitar history and have enriched source materials for future researchers and historians on the subject.

Earlier in the chapter, in the section on guitarists, it was inevitable that mention be made of the composers with whom they were closely associated. Hence, passing references were made to Mario Castelnuovo-Tedesco, Manuel Ponce, Joaquin Rodrigo, Alexander Tansman, Daniel Lesur, Pierre Petit, André Jolivet, Julian Orbon, Lennox Berkeley and Benjamin Britten. These names by no means constitute a complete list of the most significant composers for the instrument, for their numbers and efforts increase in proportion to the growing realization of the guitar's expressive potential. The following brief sketches are therefore in the nature of a supplement to the above listing.

Heitor Villa-Lobos (1887-1959), the greatest Brazilian composer of the century, proved his exceptional knowledge of the guitar in his many works for the instrument. His pieces, which include five *Choros,* five preludes, twelve etudes and a concerto for guitar and orchestra, are extremely guitaristic and ingratiating.

The Spanish master Joaquin Turina (1882-1949) has contributed much to the repertoire of the guitar. His works show the influence of his native folk music and include a sonata and a *Fandanguillo* which are popular among lovers of the guitar.

A countryman of Turina, Moreno Torroba (1891-), a prolific composer, has written a sonatina in three movements, a *Suite Castellana* and two volumes of *Pièces Caractéristiques*, to mention but a few of his numerous compositions.

Manuel de Falla wrote just one piece for guitar, but quality has made up for quantity; the *Homenaje, "Le Tombeau de Claude Debussy"* is a beautiful composition that merits a place in the guitarist's repertoire.

Many other distinguished composers have written only one important work for the guitar to date, but attention must be drawn to them because their compositions are a valuable addition to the literature. Among them are Francis Poulenc, Darius Milhaud, Frank Martin, Goffredo Petrassi, Giorgio Federico Ghedini, Henry Sauguet and Carlos Surinach. Among the twelve-tone composers are Arnold Schoenberg, Anton Webern and Ernst Krenek. Igor Stravinsky has also made use of the instrument in some of his works.[*]

The conciseness of the present book precludes any greater detail than this but it should be kept in mind that the literature for guitar has been inestimably enriched in the present century and is constantly growing.

At present, the internationalization of the guitar is virtually complete. The instrument is taught as far afield as the Americas and Egypt, Australia and Greece, Ceylon and Japan. Kimpachi Hiruma is credited with introducing the guitar to Japan upon his return from Italy in 1901. After the second World War, the instrument became incredibly popular in Japan and now the country has a great number of guitarists, teachers and guitar makers.

Almost everywhere magazines dealing with the guitar are published and available. There are, in fact, so many of these that the field of choice has become a very wide one.

The *International Guitar News* is published in England and edited by Wilfrid M. Appleby. It has subscribers in no less than sixty countries and it prints articles on guitar activities throughout the world.

The *Guitar Review*, published in New York and edited by Vladimir Bobri and Gregory d'Alessio, also has a worldwide circulation and is known for its luxurious editions.

The burgeoning of societies, associations and organizations devoted to some facet or other of guitar activity bears further witness to the universal interest in the instrument. These organizations present young guitarists in recitals, encourage study, stimulate audiences and dedicate themselves to a great variety of aims, all of which have to do with the propagation of matters pertinent to the guitar.

The number of concerts provides another index. In New York City alone, guitar recitals have multiplied ten times within the last ten years, with Andrés Segovia alone giving more than three concerts each season.

Competitions are held on both national and international levels. An especially significant competition is *La Coupe Internationale de la Guitare* held annually in Paris

---

[*]The author modestly mentions himself as a composer of numerous works for guitar.

and organized by *La Radiodiffusion-Television Francaise.* Performers and composers are invited to participate in this competition. In this way equal emphasis is given to performance and literature.

Thus, the Twentieth century so far has seen a steadily broadening and brightening horizon in guitar history, one that defies comparison with any other in the past. All the preceding centuries can be scanned as from a peak. The future seems to hold much promise and the present is the beneficiary of a rich legacy and a climate favorable to creativity and aspiration.

Epilogue

*T*he character and scope of our subject matter have imposed obligations to detail which I have attempted to fulfill within the space limitations of one volume. I have tapped archaeological, artistic, musical and historical sources in the search for facts and for evidence. To crystallize the information given in the preceding pages, I have appended a chart that traces the evolution of the guitar from 2500 B.C. to the present. A recapitulation of the guideposts in the history of the instrument may also prove helpful.

We found the earliest string instruments to be harps of two basic types; the vertical-neck harp, which attained its fullest development in Sumer by the third millenium B.C., and the bow-shaped harps, which reached a similarly advanced stage in Egypt at about the same time. The Sumerian harp exemplified by Queen Shub-Ad's instrument may have developed into a string instrument with a horizontal neck, perhaps during the latter part of the third millenium B.C. There is a strong possibility that future excavations at the Akkadian capital, Agad, will reveal evidence of such an instrument, since the Akkadians ruled this part of the world prior to the rise of Babylonia. By the beginning of the second millenium B.C., the Babylonians had string instruments with horizontal necks. The evidence is on the sculptured plaques showing such instruments played by priests.

While these developments were taking place in the Mesopotamian region, the bow-shaped harp of Egypt was undergoing a process which also led to the lowering of its neck. This process ended in the beginning of the second millenium B.C. when the neck finally became aligned to the body of the instrument in a perfectly horizontal position. The instrument found close by the mummy of Har-Mosĕ is its first surviving example.

About a century later (c. 1400 B.C.) Babylonia and other Near Eastern nations were conquered by Egypt. This event made possible the importation into Egypt of a necked string instrument undoubtedly evolved from that seen in the hands of the Babylonian priests on sculptured plaques (c. 1900 B.C.). This imported instrument was readily adopted by the Egyptians, who placed great importance on music for festive occasions and celebrations of military victories. In a relatively short time, the "new" instrument was being depicted in Egyptian art.

In Egypt, the guitar-like instrument from Babylonia came in contact with the Har-Mosĕ-type instrument and as a result underwent certain changes. In its modified form, it became even more firmly entrenched in Egyptian musical life. At some point thereafter curves appeared along the sides of its soundbox. This feature had been observed before on a Hittite instrument shown in a relief sculpture dated c. 1300 B.C. It is therefore probable that the curves on the Egyptian instrument came to being as a result of Hittite influence.

Further evolution of this instrument led to the Roman period "guitar" of c. third century A.D. Two or three centuries later it developed into the Coptic period "guitar."

At this point, the evolution of the guitar shifted from an Egyptian background to a European one, due largely to the emergence of Europe as an economic and political power.

In Europe, two trends appeared, one paralleling the other. The first of these seems to have been a completely indigenous phenomenon. The starting point is indicated by an extremely interesting instrument represented in the ninth century psalter now in Stuttgart. Although its soundbox had no curves, this instrument showed a general similarity to the guitar, particularly in the relationship of its soundbox to its neck. It appears to have retained its original form right through the medieval period, but at the same time mutants which exhibited curves seem to have developed as indicated by the guitar-shaped instruments depicted in the English St. Alban's Psalter (first quarter of the twelfth century) and by the various thirteenth and fourteenth century sculptures found in England.

The precise point at which the instrument developed clearly defined curves cannot be ascertained but certain influences may be traced to the second trend.

This trend is actually the continuation of the development which began in Egypt; hence, the curves on the sides of the soundbox had already developed long before they were observed in the instruments representing the first trend. At some time in the early Middle Ages, the Egyptian "guitar" made its way to the Mediterranean coast of Europe—probably to Provence whence it traveled to Spain, France, Italy and England. We have suggested the troubadours of Provence as being the main agents responsible for this. By the end of the twelfth century, Spanish and French churches were liberally adorned with sculptures of this instrument. The instrument by this time was both bowed and plucked. Its popularity in medieval times is demonstrated by the numerous representations in sculptures and paintings.

Sometime in the later Middle Ages, the two trends fused.

By the sixteenth century, a stricter differentiation between musical instruments took place. We finally see unquestionably modern guitars in Italy, France and Spain with four, five or six courses of double strings. The succeeding centuries witnessed the steady increase of the guitar's popularity, an increase which until the present time shows no signs of diminishing. The acceptance of the guitar on all levels of society and culture has become a hallmark of the twentieth century.

Reviewing the history of the guitar, the only unanswered question seems to be when the six single string guitar evolved. The most that can be said at present is that this took place in Italy some time in the middle of the eighteenth century. Once developed, however, it was this form of the guitar that became most widely accepted. It is the instrument for which an increasing number of serious composers have written and are writing much wonderful music, the instrument whose charm remains the delight of performers and audiences alike.

Bibliography

Ancient Near Eastern and Egyptian History and Musical Culture

Ceram, C. W. *The Secret of the Hittites*, 4th edition. New York: Alfred A. Knopf, 1958.

Champdor, Albert. *Babylon*. New York: G. P. Putnam & Sons, 1958.

Contenau, Georges. *Everyday Life in Babylon and Assyria*. London: Edward Arnold, Ltd., 1959.

Frankfort, Henri. *The Birth of Civilization in the Near East*. Bloomington, Indiana: Indiana University Press, 1954.

Hickman, Hans. *Quarante-Cinq Siècles de Musique dans L'Egypte Ancienne*. Paris: Richard-Masse, 1956.

Scott, Nora. "The Lute of the Singer Har-Mosĕ," *Bulletin of the Metropolitan Museum of Art*. New York: Metropolitan Museum of Art, 1944.

Bulletin of the Metropolitan Museum of Art. New York: Metropolitan Museum of Art, January, 1937.

Woolley, Leonard C. *Ur Excavations: The Royal Cemetery* (A Report on the Predynastic and Sargonid Graves Excavated Between 1926 and 1931), II. Great Britain: Published for the Trustees of the British Museum and the Museum of the University of Pennsylvania, 1934.

Woolley, Leonard C. *Excavations at Ur*. New York: Thomas Y. Crowell.

Medieval and Modern Musical Culture

Anderson, M. D. *Misericords.* Harmondsworth, England: Penguin Books, 1956.

Berlioz, Hector. *A treatise on modern instrumentation and orchestrations.* London: Novello Ewer & Co.

Biernath, Ernst. *Die Guitarre.* Berlin, 1907.

Bone, Philip J. *The Guitar and Mandolin,* 2nd edition. London: Schott & Co., 1954.

Buchner, Alexander. *Musical Instruments Through the Ages.* London: Spring Books.

Buek, Fritz. *Die Guitarre und Ihre Meister,* 3rd edition. Berlin: Robert Lienau, vormals Schlesinger, 1926.

Cellini, Benvenuto. *Autobiography,* translated by John A. Symonds. New York: Doubleday.

Chase, Gilbert. *The Music of Spain,* 2nd edition. New York: Dover Publications, 1959.

Hipkins, A. J. *Musical Instruments.* London: A. and C. Black, Ltd., 1921.

Prat, Domingo. *Diccionario de Guitarristas.* Buenos Aires: Romero y Fernandez.

Sachs, Curt. *The History of Musical Instruments.* New York: W. W. Norton, 1940.

Wolman, Boris L. *Guitar in Russia.* Leningrad: Musgiz, 1961.

Zuth, Josef. *Handbuch der Laute und Gitarre.* Vienna: Guberner Hierhammer, 1926.

Facsimile of Manuscripts

Brayssing, Gregoire. *Quart livre de tablature de guiterre.* Paris, 1553.

Calvi, Carlo. *Intavolatura di chitarra e chitarriglia.* Bologna: Giacomo Monti, 1646.

Corbetta, Francesco. *Varii capricii per chitarra spagnuola.* Milano: G. Bianini, 1643.

Foscarini (L'academico Caliginoso). *Il primo, secondo e terzo libro della chitarra spagnola.* c. 1630.

Fuenllana, Miguel de. *Libro de Musica para Vihuela, intitulado Orphenica Lyra.* Sevilla, 1554.

Granata, Gio. Battista. *Capricci Armonici.* Bologna, 1680. *Souavi Concenti di Sonate Musicali.* Bologna, 1659.

Guerau, Francisco. *Poema Harmonico.* Madrid: Imprenta de Manuel Ruiz de Murga, 1694.

Kremberg, Jacob. *Musicalische Bemüths Ergötzung oder Arien.* Dresden: Christoph Mathesius, 1689.

Le Roy, Adrian. *Premier Livre de Tablature de Guiterre.* Paris, 1551.

    Tiers Livre de Tablature de Guiterre. Paris, 1552.

Milan, Luys. *Libro de Musica de Vihuela de Mano Intitulado El Maestro* (Valencia, 1535), 2nd edition. Leipzig: Breitkopf & Härtel, 1927.

Pellegrini, Domenico. *Armoniosi Concerti sopra la chitarra spagnuola.* Bolognia: Giacomo Monti, 1650.

Sanz, Gaspar. *Instrucción de musica sobre la guitarra española.* Zaragoça, 1697.

Visée, Robert de. *Livre de guittarre.* Paris, 1682.

Acknowledgments

The following grateful acknowledgments are made for illustrative materials used in this volume.

Archaeological Museum. Ankara, Turkey. Plate VIII.

Ashmolean Museum. Oxford, England. Plates XXXV, XLIX, LXIII, LXIV.

Biblioteca Central. Barcelona, Spain. Plates XXII, XXXIX a

Cairo Museum. Egypt. Plate XIII.

Cleveland Museum of Art. Cleveland, Ohio. Plate XXXI.

Collection of Senor Joaquin Arcas. Barcelona, Spain. Plate XXXVII.

Collection of Vladimir M. Eitingon. New York, N. Y. Plates XLII, XLV, LXII.

Collection of William E. Hill & Son. London, England. Plates LIII, LX, LXXII, LXXIII, XCVII.

Conservatoire National de Musique. Paris, France. Plate LXXIV.

Egyptological Institute of the University of Heidelberg. Heidelberg, Germany. Plate XVIIb.

Gemeentemuseum's-Gravenhage. The Hague, Netherlands. Plates XXXIV, XLIII, LI, LXXIX, LXXX, XCV.

Horniman Museum. London, England. Plate LXXVI.

Jacquemart-Andre Museum. Paris, France. Plate XXXVI.

Louvre Museum. Paris, France. Plates III, V, VI.

Metropolitan Museum of Art. New York, N. Y. Plates IX, X, XIa, XVI, XVIIa, XXVII, LIV, LXXVII, LXXXIII, LXXXVI, LXXXVII, LXXXIX.

Musee du Conservatoire National de Musique. Paris, France. Plate XCVI.

Musei Capitolini. Rome, Italy. Plate XVIIIa.

Museo Municipal de Instrumentos. Barcelona, Spain. Plates LXXXI, LXXXII, XC, XCI, XCII, XCIII, XCIX, C.

Museum fur Völkerkunde un Vorgeschichte. Hamburg, Germany. Plate XII.

Museum of Fine Arts. Boston, Mass. Plates XLIV, LXXVIII, LXXXV.

New York Public Library. New York, N. Y. Plates XXXVIII, XL.

Oriental Institute. University of Chicago. Chicago, Ill. Plates IV, VII, XIb, XIV.

Pierpont Morgan Library. New York, N. Y. Plates XXI, XXIII.

Rijksmuseum. Amsterdam, The Netherlands. Plate LII.

Rijksmuseum. Leiden, The Netherlands. Plate XV.

Royal College of Music. London, England. Plates XLVI, XCIV.

William H. Schab Gallery. New York, N. Y. Plate XLI.

Smithsonian Institution. Washington, D. C. Plates L, LXXXIV.

Trustees of the British Museum. London, England. Plates I, II.

Tudor Copyright Photos. Suffolk, England. Plate XXIVb.

Victoria and Albert Museum. London, England. Plates XXIVa, LV, LVI, LVII, LVIII, LIX, LXXV, LXXXVIII.

Württembergische Landesbibliothek. Stuttgart, Germany. Plates XIX, XX.

Index

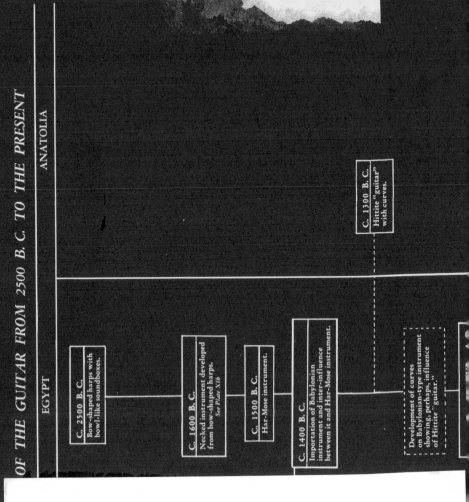

OF THE GUITAR FROM 2500 B. C. TO THE PRESENT

ANATOLIA

EGYPT

C. 2500 B. C.
Bow-shaped harps with bowl-like soundboxes.

C. 1600 B. C.
Necked instrument developed from bow-shaped harps.
See Plate XIb

C. 1500 B. C.
Har-Mose instrument.

C. 1400 B. C.
Importation of Babylonian instrument and inter-influence between it and Har-Mose instrument.

C. 1300 B. C.
Hittite "guitar" with curves.

Development of curves on Babylonian-type instrument showing, perhaps, influence of Hittite "guitar."